AT-TALAQ

A True Fashion of Talaq in Islam

RAZA ABD-AL-WAHID

Title: At-Talaq (A True Fashion Of Talaq In Islam)
Author: Raza Abd-Al-Wahid
First Edition: 2025
ISBN: 978-93-342-6355-8
Language: English
Country: Delhi (India)

Contents

Foreword

Divorce in Islam is something that, although allowed, but disliked by Allah SWT. Sadly, due to the influence of religious divisions, this important issue has become misunderstood and misused. Different groups have interpreted divorce in their own ways, often far from what Islam truly teaches. Because of these wrong understandings, harmful practices like Halaala have spread—bringing shame to the Muslim community. In this powerful and eye-opening book, Raza Abd-Al- Wahid explains the true teachings of the Prophet Muhammad (peace be upon him) with clear proofs and wisdom. He brings to light the real history of divorce in Islam, like a mirror reflecting the truth.

Anyone who reads this book will clearly see how the Qur'an explains divorce and how our beloved Prophet (peace be upon him) guided us about it. This book gives a deep and honest analysis of divorce based on the Qur'an, Hadith, and Islamic law —and invites the reader to understand the true beauty and justice of Islam.

Sayyeda Saniya Zehra Naqvi

Delhi

28th March 2025

Preface

Do we see woman Islamic scholars in fourteen hundred years of Islamic History? The answer is troublesome and tough to such extent that one would think for hours. I thought a lot about it and concluded about this piece of history that most of us ignored. We applied the rules of Islam with a very negative behavior against women. In the name of religion and rituals we overruled their choices and rights in the realm of marriage and divorce. We ignored their share of property in the house. We ignored their rights of education. We left them helpless in wretched small rooms after their husbands were dead. Who propounded this religion? None but the man himself because he has been curious for the post of divinity since early times. Those were us who applied our ego on socio-political life of woman. If we go in any of the Muslim house in the city and ask about the basic principles of Islam. We will surely get nothing but the myths on the sheet of religion. Ninety five percent of Muslim woman population does not know the ABC of their religion. They have been told not to read quranic translations otherwise they will be misguided. I observed such myths from my early age presented to me as religion, but I condemned, and you should too.

Raza Abd Al-Wahid

Delhi

27th October 2024

"To my beloved parents and wife

- The Author

CHAPTER I

The Quran and Talaq

In the name of Allah, Most Gracious, Most Merciful.

The Quran is the communication of God to mankind through his messenger Mohammad (peace be upon him). The words of Quran are primary and the most authentic source of law in Islam. The whole literature of Islamic studies is subject to the verification of the Quran's ruling. Nothing but the Quran is the supreme document to rely upon for the believers and non-believers to prove the true fashion of things. There was none but Allah SWT who guided us in the darkness and taught us the fair administration of affairs.

Allah says (65:01)

> O Prophet! When you Do divorce women, Divorce them at their Prescribed periods, And count (accurately) Their prescribed periods : And fear God your Lord : And turn them not out Of their houses, nor shall They (themselves) leave, Except in case they are Guilty of some open lewdness, Those are limits, Set by God : and any Who transgresses the limits Of God, does verily Wrong his (own) soul : Thou knowest not if Perchance God will Bring about thereafter Some new situation.

In the above-mentioned verse of Surah At-Talaq, Allah simplifies the first requisite of talaq that the woman should be in her pure days. The days of purity are when the menstrual period ends, and a woman becomes physically pure. Allah also orders to accurately count the days of menstruation. After pronouncing talaq a man pronouncing Talaq is ordered to keep his wife with him and also the wife is ordered to stay in his husband's home unless she commits open immorality. Allah also provides the procedure to prove the guilt of a person for an offence in Quran which is not the topic here. An exception has been provided as to rule not expelling the wife out of the house of husband in case of open immorality. Allah SWT points out these commands as the limits and also gives fear to those who violates his rules. In the end of this verse Allah shows his wisdom in a single line as to the chances of their rejoining in future and Allah says you do not know the situation Allah will bring about.

Allah says (65.02)

> Thus, when they fulfill Their term appointed, either take them back on equitable terms or part with them on equitable terms; And take for witness Two persons from among you, endued with justice, and establish the evidence (As) before God. Such Is the admonition given to him who believes In God and the Last Day. And for those who fear God, He (ever) prepares A way out,

When three menstrual period ends, which Allah has directed to count in previous verse Allah says either retain them or part them and directs the presence of two witnesses of good character who give their words for the sake of Allah. It is the guidance that Allah has bestowed upon his believers and Allah further says whoever keeps fear of his lord's disobedience in his heart will surely get a way in trouble.

Allah says (65:04)

> Such of your women As have passed the age Of monthly courses, for them The prescribed period, if

> ye Have any doubts, is Three months, and for those Who have no courses (It is the same) : For those who carry (Life within their wombs), Their period is until They deliver their burdens : And for those who Fear God, He will Make their path easy.

Allah prescribes time for those who do not get their periods on time to be three months or three menstrual periods and if they are pregnant then the period of Iddah extends to the delivery of the child. Allah here by ending the verse gives patience to those who believe, that their lord will make path easy for them.

- **Allah SWT further mentions Talaq in the verses of chapter two (Al-Baqarah).**

Allah says (2.226)

> For those who take an oath for abstention from their wives a waiting for four months is ordained; if then they return God is Oft Forgiving Most Merciful.

Allah SWT orders a husband who takes oath to stay away from his wife to continue his abstinence for four months and if he wants to sustain his bond during or after this period so he may keep her back with consent and they both may live together as husband and wife. The important thing to note here is if the prescribed period ends and husband and wife make their minds again to live together, they may continue their first nikah and this will be counted as one talaq.

Allah says 2:229

> A divorce is only permissible twice: after that the parties should either hold together on equitable terms or separate with kindness. It is not lawful for you (men) to take back any of your gifts (from your wives) except when both parties fear that they would

> be unable to keep the limits ordained by God. If ye (judges) do indeed fear that they would be unable to keep the limits ordained by God there is no blame on either of them if she give something for her freedom. These are the limits ordained by God; so, do not transgress them. If any do transgress the limits ordained by God such persons wrong (themselves as well as others)

This is the most misunderstood point of talaq by majority of the opinions of people in Islam. Allah SWT pronounces here that a divorce which is revocable is only permissible twice in lifetime after which they may continue their marriage but if a man pronounces third divorce it is irrevocable. It is Triple Talaq in lifetime not in three months or four months or three pronouncements at a time after which Allah SWT forbids them to get unite and mandates their separation. They may not unite unless or until the divorcee remarries to another man and the latter also divorces her in a natural way.

In the above-mentioned verse, the word "gifts" refers to the Mehr (bridal gifts) including jewelry, cloths and so on which the husband offers as a gift to his wife and to which he has no right of reclaim at the time of divorce. Indeed, it is also contrary to the moral principles of Islam that he should reclaim something which he has made over to another by way of donation or gift. As per Islamic ethics the husband ought to present a farewell gift to the woman divorced. Allah SWT has laid directions for the woman who is seeking Khula (The right of woman in demanding the dissolution of marriage) that she may return the Mahr (dowry) or reach a financial settlement with her husband. Allah SWT terrifies those who refuse to obey their lord's command they are indeed in darkness. This honorable Ayah abrogated the previous practice of Arabs in the beginning of Islam, when the man had the right to take back his divorced wife even if he had divorced her a hundred times, if she was still in her `Iddah (waiting period). This situation was harmful for the wife, and this is why Allah made the divorce thrice, where the husband is allowed to take back his wife after the first and the second divorce (as long as she is still in her `Iddah). The divorce becomes irrevocable after the third divorce.

Allah says 2:230

> And if he has divorced her [for the third time], then she is not lawful to him afterward until [after] she marries a husband other than him. And if the latter husband divorces her [or dies], there is no blame upon the woman and her former husband for returning to each other if they think that they can keep [within] the limits of Allah. These are the limits of Allah, which He makes clear to people who know.

- **People who indulge in Tehlil or Halalah were cursed.**

Imam Ahmad reported that `Abdullah bin Mas`ud said, "Allah's Messenger cursed the one who does Tahlil, the one in whose favor it is done, those who eat Riba (usury) and those who feed it (pay the usury)." At-Tirmidhi and An-Nasa'i reported this Hadith and At-Tirmidhi said, "This Hadith is Hasan." He said, "This is what is acted upon according to people of knowledge among the Companions, among whom are `Umar, `Uthman and Ibn `Umar. It was also the saying of the scholars of Fiqh among the Tabi`in (second generation of Islam). And it has been reported from `Ali, Ibn Mas`ud and Ibn `Abbas''.

In his Mustadrak, Al-Hakim reported that Nafi` said: "A man came to Ibn `Umar and asked him about a man who divorced his wife three times. Then, his brother married her to make Tahlil for his brother, without the brother knowing this fact. He then asked, "Is she allowed for the first (husband)''He said, "No, unless it is a marriage that involves desire. We used to consider this an act of adultery during the time of Allah's Messenger. 'Al-Hakim said, "This Hadith has a Sahih chain although they (Al-Bukhari and Muslim) did not record it. ''The wording of this Hadith indicates that the ruling came from the Prophet. Abu Bakr bin Abu Shaybah, Al-Jawzjani, Harb Al-Kirmani and Abu Bakr Al-Athram said that Qabisah bin Jabir said that `Umar said, "If the participants to Tahlil are brought to me, I will have them stoned.' '

Allah says (2:231)

> And when you divorce women and they have [nearly] fulfilled their term, either retain them according to acceptable terms or release them according to acceptable terms, and do not keep them, intending harm, to transgress [against them]. And whoever does that has certainly wronged himself. And do not take the verses of Allah in jest. And remember the favor of Allah upon you and what has been revealed to you of the Book and wisdom by which He instructs you. And fear Allah and know that Allah is Knowing of all things.

In this honorable verse Allah SWT says a husband may not revoke the divorce he has pronounced on his wife before the expiration of the period of waiting for the sole purpose of harassing and tormenting her. When a person revokes a divorce, God commands that this decision be prompted by a sincere desire to live together peacefully. If the intention is not present, it is better to part company in a graceful manner. Allah SWT also commemorates that it is important for muslims to remember that by teaching them the Book and Wisdom, God entrusted them with the great responsibility of guiding the world. Additionally, they should not forget that they were designated as a 'community of the middle way'and as witnesses of the virtues and the righteousness of God.

- **Freedom of woman remarrying after divorce with whomever she wills.**

Allah says (2:232)

> And when you divorce women and they have fulfilled their term, do not prevent them from remarrying their [former] husbands if they agree among themselves on an acceptable basis. That is instructed to whoever of you believes in Allah and the Last Day. That is better for you and purer, and Allah knows, and you know not.

In this verse it is clearer as crystal that, the divorced woman's relatives are instructed. When a woman has completed her waiting period. Now, she is free to remarry whomever she wants and the relatives of the divorced should not create difficulties to her. she may marry to her former husband or any other man as per her desire. Allah admonishes those by way of saying 'you know not' to those who create problems for divorced women and refuse to obey their Lord's instructions. They put their own traditions into the path of justice and give those traditions a bigger status than the command of Allah SWT.

- **In case of death of the husband.**

Allah says (2:234)

> And those who are taken in death among you and leave wives behind - they, [the wives, shall] wait four months and ten [days]. And when they have fulfilled their term, then there is no blame upon you for what they do with themselves in an acceptable manner. And Allah is [fully] Acquainted with what you do.

In this verse Allah SWT further gives directions for a woman whose husband has been expired that the waiting period for her is four months and ten days after which she may remarry as per the rule laid down in previous verses of this chain. An elderly woman (yaayisa) who can no longer have children has no waiting period and those who say that an yaayisa must observe the waiting period do not require that she isolate herself in her husband's home. The rule for a woman to stay in her husband's home is only for a divorced woman until the completion of Iddah which does not mean isolation she may go out for visit and be visited. People unfortunately confuse custom and cultural habits with Shariah rules.

- **In case when marriage is not consumed.**

Allah says (2:236)

> There is no blame upon you if you divorce women, you have not touched nor specified for them an obligation. But give them [a gift of] compensation - the wealthy according to his capability and the poor according to his capability - a provision according to what is acceptable, a duty upon the doers of good.

The same procedure will be followed which has been discussed in previous verses of this chain. further Allah SWT gives directions to pay compensation for the mental loss and suffering to the woman as per the financial capability of the husband. This principle has been adopted by the modern law and other legal systems so that justice may be served. It is mentioned as a duty of good doers in this verse.

- **Allah prescribes no waiting period for untouched wives.**

Allah says in Surah Al-Ahzab (33:49)

> O You who have believed, when you marry believing women and then divorce them before you have touched them, then there is not for you any waiting period to count concerning them. So, provide for them and give them a gracious release.

A clear ruling comes from this verse. Allah SWT makes clear as to the wives who have not been touched by their husbands are free from the obligation of waiting period. Husbands are commanded to provide them a gracious release from the bond of marriage.

- **Maintenance of widow by the family of husband after his death.**

Allah says (2:240)

> And those who are taken in death among you and leave wives behind - for their wives is a bequest: maintenance for one year without turning [them] out. But if they leave [of their own accord], then there is no blame upon you for what they do with themselves in an acceptable way. And Allah is Exalted in Might and Wise.

An instruction has been given to the family members of the husband to maintain the wife after his death for a period of one year and it has mentioned as a bequest of the wife whose husband has expired that after the death of her husband the duty to care will be performed by his family members and they will maintain her for a term of one year. In case wife leaves her matrimonial home by her consent then the family is free from any responsibility to maintain.

- **Zihaar**

Allah says (58:3)

> Those who pronounce Zihaar among you [to separate] from their wives – they are not [consequently] their mothers. Their mothers are none but those who gave birth to them. And indeed, they are saying an objectionable statement and a falsehood. But indeed, Allah is Pardoning and Forgiving.

Zihaar is an act whereby a husband compares his wife to his mother or another female relative like sister or daughter. In the age of ignorance people of Arab used to pronounce Zihaar to their wives. It was believed that Zihaar terminates marriage, but Allah SWT condemned the social evil of Zihaar and made it a sin. Allah SWT removed the doubt of Zihaar and cleared the point that Zihaar does not result in divorce.

CHAPTER II

The Hadith and Talaq

A short introduction of the meaning of hadith is necessary, to provide here. The word Hadith means ’tale 'or ’communication 'not only are communications of those who embraced Islam, but also historical information whether secular or religious is called Hadith. In various books of Hadith, the word ’hadith' has been used by the narrators while telling of some past event. Abu Huraira asks ’Shall I regale you with a hadith from your hadiths, O community of the Ansar? and then tells them a story of an episode in the conquest of Mecca. In simple, a modern Muslim knows Hadith as the saying of the Prophet.

The narrations of the Prophet Muhammad peace be upon him were memorized by his pious companions and were reduced to writing by latter generations. The authenticity of a Hadith remained a big concern for Hadith compilers since early times and so far. Despite great care a big number of fabricated hadiths were attributed to Prophet Muhammad and became a part of Islamic society. So was the situation of Talaq in Hadith literature. Diverse views may be seen as to the procedure of Talaq in various hadiths some of which follow Quran’s ruling and some not.

There are some principles on which we rely upon while checking the authenticity of a Hadith.

Principles

- The concerned hadith must be a part of a continuous chain of narrators.
- The concerned hadith must be transmitted by reliable narrators.

- The links of the narrators.
- The concerned hadith must not be contradictory to any other hadith.
- The content (matn) of the concerned hadith must not be contradictory to the Quran's ruling.

There are six books of hadiths in Sunni Islam which are acknowledged by majority of Sunni scholars.

1. Sahih al Bukhari, collected by Imam Bukhari (d. 870), includes 7275 ahadith.
2. Sahih Muslim, collected by Muslim b. al-Hajjaj (d. 875), includes 9200 ahadith.
3. Sunan Nasa'i, collected by an-Nasa'i (d. 915).
4. Sunan Abu Dawood, collected by Abu Dawood (d. 888).
5. Jami at-Tirmidhi, collected by al-Tirmidhi (d. 892).
6. Sunan ibn Majah, collected by Ibn Majah (d. 887).

And there are many other books of hadiths like Musnad Ahmad, Muwatta Malik, Sahih Al Jami, Mustadrak al Hakim, Ibn Hibban, Mishkat, Musand Abi Dawud Tayalisi, Muajjam at Tabrini kabeer, Muajjam e Tabrani Ausad, Maujam e Tabrani Saghreer, Musnaf Abdur Razzaq, sunan Darmi, Darqutni, Shubul Eeman Baihaiqi, As Sunan Al-Kubra, Ibn Khuzaima, Targheeb wal Tahreeb etc.

Only those hadiths which act as per Quran's ruling in the matter of talaq are being mentioned here. Following the principle of non-contradiction with Quran all other hadiths which are not in line with the Quran's ruling stand dis-affirmed.

- **Pronouncement of three Talaq at a time.**

> Makhramah narrated that his father said: "I heard Mahmud bin Labid say: 'The Messenger of Allah was told about a man who had divorced his wife with three simultaneous divorces. He stood up angrily and

said: Is the Book of Allah being toyed with while I am still among you? Then a man stood up and said: 'O Messenger of Allah, shall I kill him?'"

Sunan an-Nasa'i 3401

Ibn 'Abbas (Allah be pleased with them) reported that the (pronouncement) of three divorces during the lifetime of Allah's Messenger (may peace be upon him) and that of Abu Bakr and two years of the caliphate of Umar (Allah be pleased with him) (was treated) as one. But Umar b. Khattab (Allah be pleased with him) said: Verily the people have begun to hasten in the matter in which they are required to observe respite. So, if we had imposed this upon them, and he imposed it upon them.

Sahih Muslim 3491

Abu Sahba' said to Ibn 'Abbas (Allah be pleased with them): Do you know that three (divorces) were treated as one during the lifetime of Allah's Apostle (may peace be upon him), and that of Abu Bakr, and during three (years) of the caliphate of Umar (Allah be pleased with him)?Ibn Abbas (Allah be pleased with them) said: Yes.

Sahih Muslim 3492

Abu al-Sahba'said to Ibn 'Abbas: Enlighten us with your information whether the three divorces (pronounced at one and the same time) were not treated as one during the lifetime of Allah's Messenger (may peace be upon him) and Abu Bakr. He said: It was in fact so, but when during the caliphate of 'Umar (Allah be pleased with him) people began to pronounce divorce frequently, he allowed them to do so (to treat pronouncements of three divorces in a single breath as one).

Sahih Muslim 3493

The above mentioned four hadiths clarify the tradition regarding Triple Talaq during the lifetime of Prophet Muhammad (peace be upon him)and even after the demise of Prophet the same tradition was prevalent in Muslim society as instructed in the Quran. Above hadiths also clear that Umar (Allah be pleased with him) made an administrative decision in the third or fourth year of his rule as caliph to maintain Islamic law and order. It was an administrative step to curb the situation of negligence in taking the decision of Talaq. Umar (Allah be pleased with him) made no change in the ruling of the Quran. Triple Talaq was considered as one during the lifetime of Muhammad peace be upon him and his companions as well. There is nothing like Triple Talaq in one pronouncement or in thrice in three months in Islam, rather it is thrice in lifetime.

- **Triple Talaq in one pronouncement or three in three menstruation period will be counted as one Talaq.**

Narrated Al-Hasan: The sister of Ma'qil bin Yasar was married to a man and then that man divorced her and remained away from her till her period of the 'Iddah expired. Then he demanded for her hand in marriage, but Ma'qil got angry out of pride and haughtiness and said, "He kept away from her when he could still retain her, and now he demands her hand again?" So, Ma'qil disagreed to remarry her to him. Then Allah revealed: 'When you have divorced women and they have fulfilled the term of their prescribed period, do not prevent them from marrying their (former) husbands.' (2.232) So the Prophet (ﷺ) sent for Ma'qil and recited to him

> (Allah's order) and consequently Ma'qil gave up his pride and haughtiness and yielded to Allah's order.

Sahih al-Bukhari 5331

If it is Talaq thrice in three months or three menstruation period so why Prophet Muhammad (peace be upon him) recited Allah's order in verse (2.232) of Quran for Ma'qil, that after completing Iddah period, it is the right of husband he can keep his wife if both agree but husband has only two chances to do so in his lifetime. If he divorces her thrice than she will not be lawful for him. The above hadiths make it clear that nothing exits like three divorces during Iddah with a gap of one month or one menstruation period. Only one divorce will be counted as valid for three or four months until she completes her three-menstruation period, thereafter he may keep her in marriage or leave her.

> Fatimah bint Qais said: "I came to the Prophet and said: 'I am the daughter of Ali Khalid and my husband, so and so, sent word to me divorcing me. I asked his family for provision and shelter, but they refused.' They said: 'O Messenger of Allah, he sent word to her divorcing her thrice.'" She said: "The Messenger of Allah said: 'The woman is still entitled to provision and shelter if the husband can still take her back.'"

In case of Fatimah bin Qais, Prophet Muhammad (peace be upon him) ordered to the family of the husband to provide shelter for wife even if she was divorced thrice. The above incident shows that three pronouncements at a time had no effect in the eyes of our beloved Prophet.

Sunan an-Nasa'i 3403

> It was narrated from Ibn Tawus, from his father, that Abu As-Sahba' came to Ibn 'Abbas and said: "O Ibn 'Abbas! Did you not know that the threefold divorce during the time of the Messenger of Allah and Abu Bakr, and during the early part of 'Umar's Caliphate, used to be counted as one divorce?" He said: "Yes."

Sunan an-Nasa'i 3406

> Nafi'said: When Ibn 'Umar was asked about person who had given three divorces, he said, "Would that you gave one or two divorces, for the Prophet (ﷺ) ordered me to do so. If you give three divorces, then she cannot be lawful for you until she has married another husband (and is divorced by him)."

Sahih al-Bukhari 5264

In this hadith Umar himself desires that one should pronounce divorce one or two times, and the Prophet ordered to do so. How Umar (Allah be pleased with him) may promote frequent divorcing among the people while he was ordered by Prophet in the matter of his own son Abdullah ibn Umar.

> Narrated `Abdullah bin `Umar: that he had divorced his wife while she was menstruating during the lifetime of Allah's Messenger (ﷺ). `Umar bin Al-Khattab asked Allah's Messenger (ﷺ) about that. Allah's Messenger (ﷺ) said, "Order him (your son) to take her back and keep her till she is clean and then to wait till she gets her next period and becomes clean again, whereupon, if he wishes to keep her, he can do so, and if he wishes to divorce her he can divorce her before having sexual intercourse with her; and that is the prescribed period which Allah has fixed for the women meant to be divorced."

Sahih al-Bukhari 5251

Umar’s boldness in relation to the Islamic Shariah is a well-known thing to the Islamic world. His character as we remember today never allows us to believe that Umar (Allah be pleased with him) changed the ruling of Quran regarding Talaq.

The above hadith follows the ruling of Quran 2:229 in which Allah SWT directed about Talaq to be a reversible opportunity available only for two times in life after which the husband cannot revoke the decision and Allah SWT frees both from their responsibilities towards each other. Umar also mentioned that Prophet ordered for the same.

- **Pronouncement of Talaq in anger**

  Muhammad ibn Ubayd ibn Abu Salih who lived in Ayliya said:

  I went out with Adi ibn Adi al-Kindi till we came to Mecca. He sent me to Safiyyah's daughter of Shaybah who remembered a tradition (that she had heard) from Aisha. She said: I heard Aisha say: I heard the Messenger of Allah (ﷺ) say: There is no divorce or emancipation in case of constraint or duress (ghalaq).

  Abu Dawud said: I think ghalaq means anger.

The issue of Talaq in anger is further explained in chapter three of this book.

Sunan Abi Dawud 2193

- **Return of Mehr in case of Khul.**

  Narrated Ibn `Abbas: The wife of Thabit bin Qais came to the Prophet (ﷺ) and said, "O Allah’s

Messenger (ﷺ)! I do not blame Thabit for defects in his character or his religion, but I, being a Muslim, dislike to behave in un-Islamic manner (if I remain with him)." On that Allah's Messenger (ﷺ) said (to her), "Will you give back the garden which your husband has given you (as Mahr)?" She said, "Yes." Then the Prophet (ﷺ) said to Thabit, "O Thabit! Accept your garden and divorce her once."

Sahih al-Bukhari 5273 and Sahih al-Bukhari 5276

Islam also gives to the woman a right to get out of the marriage if she so desires, such right of the wife is known as khula. In case when a wife seeks khula the wife has to return the amount/gift of mahr to the husband.

- **Oath of Lian (**invoking curse**), and divorce.**

Narrated `Abdullah: An Ansari man accused his wife (of committing illegal sexual intercourse). The Prophet (ﷺ) made both takes the oath of Lian and separated them from each other (by divorce).

Sahih al-Bukhari 5306

Narrated Ibn `Abbas: Hilal bin Umaiyya accused his wife of illegal sexual intercourse and came to the Prophet (ﷺ) to bear witness (against her), (taking the oath of Lian). The Prophet (ﷺ) was saying, "Allah knows that either of you is a liar. Will anyone of you repent (to Allah)?" Then the lady got up and gave her witness.

Sahih al-Bukhari 5307

Narrated Sa`id bin Jubair: I asked Ibn `Umar, "(What is the verdict if) a man accuses his wife of illegal sexual intercourse?" Ibn `Umar said, "The Prophet

(ﷺ) separated (by divorce) the couple of Bani Al-Ajlan, and said, (to them), 'Allah knows that one of you two is a liar; so, will one of you repent? 'But both refused. He again said, 'Allah knows that one of you two is a liar; so, will one of you repent? 'But both refused. So, he separated them by divorce." (Aiyub, a sub-narrator said: `Amr bin Dinar said to me, "There is something else in this Hadith which you have not mentioned. It goes thus: The man said, 'What about my money (i.e. the Mahr that I have given to my wife)?' It was said, 'You have no right to restore any money, for if you have spoken the truth (as regards the accusation), you have also consummated your marriage with her; and if you have told a lie, you are less rightful to have your money back.' ")

Sahih al-Bukhari 5311

Allah SWT also mentions Lian in verses 6-9 of chapter 24.

> And those who accuse their wives [of adultery] and have no witnesses except themselves - then the witness of one of them [shall be] four testimonies [swearing] by Allah that indeed, he is of the truthful.
>
> And the fifth [oath will be] that the curse of Allah be upon him if he should be among the liars.
>
> But it will prevent punishment from her if she gives four testimonies [swearing] by Allah that indeed, he is of the liars.
>
> And the fifth [oath will be] that the wrath of Allah be upon her if he was of the truthful.

Quran provides what one should do in case when he is encountered with the situation of adultery. When a husband accuses his wife of adultery, he must prove it by way of witnesses and if there are no witnesses except the husband so he will take four oaths, and the wife will also do the same. Fifth oath will be in the form of the curse upon the lair. Indeed, Islam resolves the issues among individuals by way of Quran. Quran is not only a source of guidance and mercy but also a complete code of socio-political laws of society.

- **Period of Iddah for a pregnant woman ends after delivery.**

> Narrated Um Salama: (the wife of the Prophet) A lady from Bani Aslam, called Subai'a, become a widow while she was pregnant. Abu As-Sanabil bin Ba'kak demanded her hand in marriage, but she refused to marry him and said, "By Allah, I cannot marry him unless I have completed one of the two prescribed periods." About ten days later (after having delivered her child), she went to the Prophet (ﷺ) and he said (to her), "You can marry now."

Sahih al-Bukhari 5318

> Narrated Al-Miswer bin Makhrama: Subai'a Al-Aslamiya gave birth to a child a few days after the death of her husband. She came to the Prophet and asked permission to remarry, and the Prophet (ﷺ) gave her permission, and she got married.

Sahih al-Bukhari 5320

> 'Ubaidullah b. 'Abdullah b. 'Utba (b. Mas'ud) reported that his father wrote to Umar b. 'Abdullah b al Arqam al-Zuhri that he would go to Subai'ah bint al-Hirith al-Aslamiyya (Allah be pleased with her) and ask her about a verdict from him which Allah's Messenger (may peace be upon him) gave her when

she had asked that from him (in regard to the termination of 'Idda at the birth of a child) 'Umar b. Abdullah wrote to 'Abdullah b.'Utba informing him that Subai'ah had told him that she had been married to Sa'd b. Khaula and he belonged to the tribe of Amir b. Lu'ayy, and was one of those who participated in the Battle of Badr, and he died in the Farewell Pilgrimage and she had been in the family way at that time. And much time had not elapsed that she gave birth to a child after his death and when she was free from the effects of childbirth, she embellished herself for those who had to give proposals of marriage. Abd al-Sunabil b. Ba'kak (from Banu 'Abd al-Dar) came to her and said: What is this that I see you embellished; perhaps you are inclined to marry, By Allah, you cannot marry unless four months and ten days (of 'Idda are passed). When he said that. I dressed myself, and as it was evening I came to Allah's Messenger (may peace be upon him) and asked him about it, and he gave me a religious verdict that I was allowed to marry when I had given birth to a child and asked me to marry if I so liked. Ibn Shihab said: I do not find any harm fur her in marrying when she has given birth to a child even when she is bleeding (after the birth of the child) except that her husband should not go near her until she is purified.

Sahih Muslim 3536

Quran mentions in 65:04 as to the end of the Iddah after the delivery of child. It is evident from above-mentioned hadiths that the period of iddah for a pregnant woman ends after the delivery of the child. The above-mentioned hadiths make it more visible by telling factual situation and the manner adopted by Prophet Muhammad in this regard.

- **Keeping a widow isolated, ill-treated, in a wretched small room is not Islam.**

> I (Humaid) said to Zainab, "What does 'throwing a globe of dung when one year had elapsed' mean?" Zainab said, "When a lady was bereaved of her husband, she would live in a wretched small room and put on the worst clothes she had and would not touch any scent till one year had elapsed. Then she would bring an animal, e.g. a donkey, a sheep or a bird and rub her body against it. The animal against which she would rub her body would scarcely survive. Only then she would come out of her room, whereupon she would be given a globe of dung which she would throw away and then she would use the scent she liked or the like."

Sahih al-Bukhari 5337

> Jabir b. 'Abdullah (Allah be pleased with them) reported: My maternal aunt was divorced, and she intended to pluck her dates. A person scolded her for having come out (during the period of 'Idda). She came to Allah's Prophet (may peace be upon him.) and he said: Certainly, you can pluck (dates) from your palm trees, for perhaps you may give charity or do an act of kindness.

Sahih Muslim 3535

In Pre-Islamic Arabia, the era that we know as Daur e Jihalat, widows were ill-treated and were kept in small rooms for a period of one year after their husbands' death. Islam opposed such practices of people and provided woman an equal status in society. even in present, a big number of people have continued adopting the same behavior with the widows which is nothing but ignorance and is a part of devil's code.

Allah says (2:208)

O Believers, enter completely into Islam and do not follow in" the footsteps of Satan, for he is your avowed enemy.

CHAPTER III

A Perusal of Sunni Fiqh and Talaq

Fiqh is a branch of Islamic Studies which means the knowledge of legal thoughts of Islam. Sunni jurists have laid down different opinions as to the concept of talaq as per their analysis of the subject. There are four most followed schools of legal thought in Sunni Fiqh i.e. the Hanafi School, the Maliki School, the Shafi'i School, the Hanbali School. These schools of Fiqh are normally based on, addressing Ibadaat, religious obligations and prohibitions (such as prayer and fasting), muʿamālāt (social life issues) which includes family law (example: regulation of marriage and divorce), inheritance, property and contracts obligations; and other areas such as criminal matters, transfer of power and governance, and legitimacy and regulation of warfare. However, it would be wrong to suggest that there are only four schools of thought. There have passed people in every century who were great Islamic Scholars and even in present many are born but this book mentions only most followed schools of thought.

The Hanafi School and Talaq

Abu Hanifa An Nauman ibn Thabit was the founder of Hanafi School. He was born in Kufa (77 A.H) and died in Baghdad. Most of the works of Abu Hanifa were composed by his two disciples i.e. Imam Yusuf and Imam Muhammad al-Shaybani. Al Fiqh Al Akbar, Kitab Al-Aathar, Musnad Abi Hanifa, Al-Asl (Al-Mabsoot) are major books of Hanafi Fiqh.

Imam Muhammad writes on page 244 in his book Kitab-ul-Athaar Urdu version.

> Abu Hanifa informed us that a man came to ibn Abbas and said that he had pronounced triple talaq unto his wife, on this ibn Abbas replied one of you indulges himself in foul smelling then comes to us , go you have disobeyed your lord and your wife is forbidden unto you so long as she remarries to another man and get divorced and comes to you again.

After mentioning above-noted hadith Imam Muhammad says that "same stands correct for us and Imam Abu Hanifa had the same opinion that triple talaq is valid".

On the one hand we say something is haram and on the other hand result of the same is valid. Half cooked stories have always been narrated by people, and they may be seen in various religious literature in the world. Islam never gave birth to corruption in human morals rather it provided the path to ease human interactions and no man has authority to unease them.

Another hadith from Sahih Muslim **3491** where ibn Abbas himself reported: -

> Ibn 'Abbas (Allah be pleased with them) reported that the (pronouncement) of three divorces during the lifetime of Allah's Messenger (may peace be upon him) and that of Abu Bakr and two years of the caliphate of Umar (Allah be pleased with him) (was treated) as one. But Umar b. Khattab (Allah be pleased with him) said: Verily the people have begun to hasten in the matter in which they are required to observe respite. So, if we had imposed this upon them, and he imposed it upon them.

A hadith is mentioned here also discussed in the previous chapter from Sunan an-Nasa'i 3401.

> Makhramah narrated that his father said: "I heard Mahmud bin Labid say: 'The Messenger of Allah was told about a man who had divorced his wife with three simultaneous divorces. He stood up angrily and said: Is the Book of Allah being toyed with while I am still among you? Then a man stood up and said: 'O Messenger of Allah, shall I kill him? '"

For Prophet Muhammad (peace be upon him) going against the Quran's ruling was equal to play with the guidance of Allah. After the demise of the Prophet (peace be upon him) Umar b. Khattab as discussed in the previous chapter took a preventive step to curb the same situation. People of Arab started playing with the manner of Talaq they used to pronounce multiple talaq at once as to prevent such act and to punish such offenders Umar being a ruler imposed a law of *Riyasat* against them. However, it is clearer than crystal and confirmed from various authentic hadiths that pronouncement of triple talaq or more than three at once was treated as one in the time of Prophet Muhammad (peace be upon him). Multiple hadiths have been mentioned in the previous chapter. If we consider some of the opinions of our learned jurists with regard to multiple pronouncements of talaq at once or what they call talaq e bidda' being valid so no authentic proof is found to confirm it. Despite being the most popular in Muslim world somewhere or at some point Hanafi Fiqh failed to provide a clean version of talaq to the Muslims.

Imam Abu Hanifa believed that a talaq by triple pronouncement does count because the reason has diminished due to sin, so the divorce counts as such, as a punishment to the husband and as a deterrent to committing the sin. (al-Mughni by Ibn Qudaamah, 7/289.)

However, Imam Abu Hanifa's belief validating pronouncement of triple talaq may be supposed as a punishment of wrongdoers as per the order of Umar bin Khattab (May Allah be pleased with him) but people of later generation turned it into a very rigid sense.

While applying a hadith and deriving rulings from it a jurist must consider the *site or place* where the event happened and the *occasion* where such act was commanded or approved by Prophet Muhammad. Merely copying the Arabic society of 7th century and pasting it in place of 21st century is not following *Sunnah* or *Quran*. The Arabic society was not the society of angels rather there were people as well who disobeyed *Quran* and opposed Prophet Muhammad so as to obtain something religious from the events of their time and to know how they behaved when they met such incidents one should take the account of their words reasonably whether these words have been transmitted properly without errors or they have put a wrong interpretation of things.

The Maliki School and Talaq

Mālik ibn Anas ibn Mālik ibn Abī ʻĀmir al-Aṣbaḥ popularly known as Imam Malik was a Medinan jurist and the founder of Maliki Fiqh in Madina. Imam malik was born in early eighth century around 90 years A.H. In the times of Imam Malik Madina al-Munawarra was flourishing with the great scholars who were the direct inheritors of the knowledge of the Companions, may Allah be pleased with them. Works of Imam Malik includes Al-Mudawwana al-Kubra and Al-Muwatta.

Imam Malik mentioned various hadiths in his Muwatta about the tradition of talaq in Arabic society.

> Yaḥyā related to me from Mālik from Nāfiʻ that ʻAbdullāh ibn ʻUmar said, "When a man divorces his wife and she begins her third period, she is free from him, and he is free from her."

Mālik said, "This is how things are done among us."

Yaḥyā related to me from Mālik from Yaḥyā ibn Sa'īd from a man of the Anṣār that his wife asked him for a divorce, and he said to her, "When you have had your period, then tell me." When she had her period, she told him. He said, "When you are purified then tell me." When she was purified, she told him, and he divorced her.

Malik said, "This is the best of what I have heard about it."

The two arbiters

Yahya related to me from Malik that he had heard that 'Ali ibn Abi Talib said about the two arbiters about whom Allah, the Exalted, says, "If you fear a breach between a couple, send an arbiter from his people and an arbiter from her people. If the couple desire to put things right, Allah will bring about a reconciliation between them. Allah is All-Knowing, All-Aware" (4:35) that both separation and joining were overseen by the two of them. **Malik said, "That is the best of what I have heard from the people of knowledge. Whatever the two arbiters say concerning separation or joining is taken into consideration."**

The above-noted hadith from Muwatta of Imam Malik brings into light how separation and joining used to be done in their time. The hadith signifies the role of two arbiters in the termination and rejoining of marriage contract.

Yahya related to me from Malik that Ibn Shihāb said that he had heard Sa'īd ibn al-Musayyab, Ḥumayd ibn ‘Abd ar-Raḥmān ibn ‘Awf, ‘Ubaydullāh ibn ‘Abdullah ibn ‘Utba ibn Masu'd, and Sulayman ibn Yasār all say that they had heard Abū Hurayra say that he had heard ‘Umar ibn al-Khaṭṭāb say, “If a woman is divorced by her husband once or twice, and he leaves her until she is free to marry and she marries another husband and he dies or divorces her, and then she re-marries her first husband, she is with him according to what remains of her divorce (i.e. there is only one or two divorces left).”

Malik said, “That is what is done among us and there is no dispute about it.”

Yahya related to me from Malik from Thābit ibn al-Aḥnaf that he married an umm walad of ‘Abd ar-Raḥmān ibn Zayd ibn alKhaṭṭāb. He said, “‘Abdullāh ibn ‘Abd ar-Raḥmān ibn Zayd ibn alKhaṭṭāb summoned me and I went to him. I came in upon him and there were whips and two iron fetters placed there, and two of his slaves whom he had made to sit there. He said, ‘Divorce her, or, by Him by whom one swears, I will do such-and-such to you!’ I said, ‘It is divorcing a thousand times.’ Then I left him and saw ‘Abdullah ibn ‘Umar on the road to Makka and I told him about my situation. ‘Abdullah ibn ‘Umar was furious, and said, ‘That is not a divorce, and she is not unlawful for you, so return to your home.’ I was still not at ease, so I went to ‘Abdullah ibn az-Zubayr who was the governor of Makka at that time. I told him about my situation and what ‘Abdullāh ibn ‘Umar had said to me. ‘Abdullāh ibn az-Zubayr said to me, ‘She is not unlawful for you, so return to your home,’ and he wrote to Jābir ibn al-Aswad az-Zuhrī who was the governor of Madina and ordered him to punish ‘Abdullah ibn ‘Abd ar-Raḥmān and to make him leave me and my family alone. I went to Madīna

> and Ṣafiyya, the wife of ‘Abdullah ibn ‘Umar, fitted out my wife so that she could bring her to my house with the knowledge of ‘Abdullāh ibn ‘Umar. Then I invited ‘Abdullāh ibn ‘Umar on the day of my wedding to the wedding feast and he came.”

A person of sound judgment may easily understand the massage in the above-noted hadith. There are two points one is divorcing in fear or coercion or undue influence which has no value neither in talaq nor in nikah. The practice of persuading daughters and sons to do Talaq and Nikah by using force or threats is completely against Quran and Sunnah but the same is prevalent in Muslim society at present as well. The second thing reveals the fact that multiple pronouncements of talaq at once has nothing to do with Islam.

> Yahya related to me from Malik that ‘Abdullah ibn Dinar said, “I heard ‘Abdullah ibn ‘Umar recites from the Qur’ān, ‘O Prophet! When you divorce women, divorce them at the beginning of their ‘iddah.’” (65:1)
>
> **Malik said, “He meant by that to make one pronouncement of divorce at the beginning of each period of purity.”**

What remains unfold after this hadith about the tradition of Talaq. Talaq is one pronouncement at a time since early times and one such pronouncement should be preceded by sound mind, pre-consideration and presence of two witnesses.

As per need kohl or some other cure for eyes may be applied during period of Idda ‘.

> Zaynab said, “I went to the house of Zaynab bint Jaḥsh, the wife of the Prophet, when her brother had

died. She called for perfume and put some on and said, 'By Allah! I have no need of perfume, but I heard the Messenger of Allah , say, "It is not lawful for a woman who trusts in Allah and the Last Day to abstain from adornment in mourning for someone who has died for more than three nights, except for four months and ten days for a husband."

Yahya related to me from Malik that he had heard that Umm Salama, the wife of the Prophet said to a woman in mourning for her husband whose eyes were troubling her, and the pain had become severe, "Apply jilā' kohl at night and wipe it off in the day."

Yahya related to me from Malik that he had heard that Sālim ibn 'Abdullāh and Sulaymān ibn Yasār said that if a woman whose husband had died feared that an inflammation of her eyes might affect her sight or that some complaint might befall her, she should put kohl on and seek a remedy with kohl or some other cure even if it had perfume in it.

Malik said, "If there is a necessity, the din of Allah is ease."

The Hanbali School and Talaq

Ahmad ibn Hanbal was born in Baghdad (163 AH). He was a prominent Muslim theologian, jurist, and martyr for his beliefs. He is best known for compiling the Musnad, a comprehensive collection of the sayings and traditions of the Prophet Muhammad, organized by isnad. Additionally, he established the Hanbali school, recognized as the most traditionalist among the four main schools of Islamic law. His teachings significantly impacted influential figures such as the theologian Ibn Taymiyyah from the 13th to 14th centuries, as well as the Wahhabi and Salafi reform movements.

- **Not an obligation to divorce upon parental request.**

> Sindi reported: A man asked Abu Abdullah, Imam Ahmad, "My father has ordered me to divorce my wife." Ahmad said, "Do not divorce her." He said, "Did not Umar command his son Abdullah to divorce his wife?" Ahmad said, "Is your father like Umar, may Allah be pleased with him?"
>
> Ibn Muflih said, "If his father commands him to divorce his wife, it is not an obligation to do so as mentioned by most of our scholars."
>
> **al-Adab al-Shar'iyah 1/447**

It is often seen that a person divorces his wife on the direction of his father or mother or any other person of his family thinking it to be a religious act. Allah SWT does not allow in any manner to obey such directions of amoral nature. Those who impose such amoral directions to their daughters and sons are sinners and lawbreakers. In Sahiḥ al-Bukhārī 7144, Sahiḥ Muslim 1839 the Prophet peace be upon him said,

> If they command sinful disobedience, then there is no listening or obedience to them.

- **View of Ibn Taymiyyah (Hanbali) about triple pronouncement of talaq at once.**

Ibn Taymiyah al-Hanbali was born in, 661 AH in Haran, which is now in Eastern Turkey, near the border of northern Iraq. His family had long been renowned for its learning, among his teachers, was Shams ud-Din Al-Maqdisi, first Hanbali Chief

Justice of Syria following the reform of the judiciary by Baibars. The number of Ibn Taimiyah's teachers exceeds two hundred. Ibn Taimiyah was barely seventeen, when Qadi Al-Maqdisi authorized him to issue Fatwa (legal verdict). Qadi remembered with pride that it was he who had first permitted an intelligent and learned man like Ibn Taimiyah to give Fatwa. At the same age, he started delivering lectures. When he was thirty, he was offered the office of Chief Justice, but refused, as he could not persuade himself to follow the limitations imposed by the authorities. Imam Ibn Taimiyah's education was essentially that of a Hanbali theologian and jurisconsult. But to his knowledge of early and classical Hanbalism, he added not only that of the other schools of jurisprudence but also that of other literature. He had an extensive knowledge of Quran, Sunnah, Greek philosophy, Islamic history, and religious books of others, as is evident from the variety of the books he wrote.

Ibn Taymiyyah, held the view that pronouncing three divorces (talaq) at once should be considered as a single divorce, not three, based on the early practice and the principle of avoiding hardship. Ibn Taymiyyah and scholars like Ibn al-Qayyim argued that during the time of the Prophet Muhammad (peace be upon him) and the early caliphs, triple divorces were treated as a single divorce. They believed that the practice of treating triple divorces as irrevocable would lead to unnecessary hardship and complications for individuals and families. Ibn Taymiyyah reasoned (718 AH) that, since violation of an oath in the name of God requires the prescribed expiation in the Qur'an, so too violation of a divorce oath requires expiation, not the actual dissolution of marriage.

- **View of Ibn Qayyim (Hanbali) about triple pronouncement of talaq at once.**

Muhammad ibn Abu Bakr (more commonly known as Ibn Qayyim or Ibn Qayyim al-Jawziyyah) (691 AH- 751 AH) was a famous Sunni Islamic jurist, commentator on the Quran, astronomer, chemist, philosopher, psychologist, scientist and theologian. Although he is commonly referred to as "the scholar of the heart," given his extensive works pertaining to human behavior and ethics, Ibn Qayyim's scholarship was focused on the sciences of Hadith and Fiqh.

Imam Ibn Al-Qayyim said: If the devil's whispers cause a person to say things which aren't by his choice, then the verdicts of his actions are dismissed. Ibn al-Qayyim also addressed the issue of divorce pronounced in a state of anger, stating that if a person is not aware of what he is saying due to intense anger, the divorce may not take place.

Allah says (7:150)

> "And when Musa (Moses) returned to his people, angry and grieved, he said: "What an evil thing is that which you have done (i.e. worshiping the calf) during my absence. Did you hasten and go ahead as regards the matter of your Lord (you left His worship)?" And he threw down the Tablets and seized his brother by (the hair of) his head and dragged him towards him. Harun (Aaron) said: "O son of my mother! Indeed, the people judged me weak and were about to kill me, so make not the enemies rejoice over me, nor put me amongst the people who are Zalimun (wrongdoers)."

Ibn Al-Qayyim mentioned that the evidence from this verse which supports divorcing while angry is invalid is Musa was propelled by anger to throw the Tablets which Allah wrote, there was no benefit for him or the children of Israel in this action. Moreover, it was his fit of fury which caused him to pull his brother Harun by his beard. Therefore, Allah did not blame or hold him responsible for his actions. Whenever anger results in the person doing an action outside of his ability to control, then this action is not attributed to that person.

Allah says (1:225)

> Allah will not call you to account for that which is unintentional in your oaths, but He will call you to account for that which your hearts have earned. And Allah is Oft-Forgiving, Most-Forbearing.

Imam Ibn Al-Qayyim said: a person is called to account for what he says based on what his heart intends. Whatever is said without the heart's intention as in a state of fury or drunkenness is not from the intention of the heart.

Uthman ibn ‘Affan may Allah be pleased with him rejected the divorce pronounced by an intoxicated person. There’s no known difference of opinion among the other companions regarding his view. Abdul Malik Al-Maymoni said: I used to believe that divorce carried out by an intoxicated person was acceptable until I became aware of the proofs, then I changed my position that it’s unacceptable.

The Shafi'i School and Talaq

Imam Shafi’i was born in the year 150 AH in Ghaza, Palestine. It was the same year in which Imam Abu Hanifah had passed away. He lost his father during infancy and was raised by his mother under very poor circumstances. Fearing the waste of his son’s lineage, his mother decided to move to Mecca where their relatives lived. Imam was very young at that time. It is quoted by some scholars that he was two years old when his mother migrated to Mecca. Therefore, he spent his formative years acquiring religious education in the cities of Mecca and Medina. There are three books related to Imam Shafi 'i viz. Al-Risala, Kitab Al-Umm, Musnad ash-Shafi'i.

Imam Shafi'i considered triple talaq as permissible and not an innovation (bid'ah).

In Sunni Islam, there is a consensus (ijma) that triple talaq is valid. Abu Hanifa and Malik ibn Anas considered it irrevocable despite its illegality. Al-Shafi'i considered it permissible, and Ahmad ibn Hanbal considered it to be valid.

During the life of above-said Imams, the rulers of Muslim world were from the Umayyad Caliphate and later, the Abbasid Caliphate. Since there was a well-established Muslim Riyasat which required a system of rules for punishment and justice just like a modern nation requires penal codes. Penal Punishments were meant for offenders and were circumstantial. An example of penal punishment is Rajm (stoning to death). Rajm was a prevalent form of penal punishment during and after the Prophet era. Penal Punishments were sentenced to those who were habitual offenders of fornication (consensual or forced), dacoity, murder, etc. In the time of Umar bin Khattab a need was felt to impose a law for those who were habitual offenders of pronouncing multiple divorces at a time so as a penal punishment of triple pronouncement of Talaq was made effective. This was the consensus/Ijma of four Sunni Imams about Triple Talaq as a valid penal punishment, but the concept was broadly misunderstood by the later generations.

- **Divorce (talaq) by one who is drunk.**

Allah says (interpretation of the meaning):

> "O you who believe! Approach not As-Salat (the prayer) when you are in a drunken state until you

> know (the meaning) of what you utter" [an-Nisa' 4:43].

Here Allah, may He be glorified, states that the word of one who is drunk does not count for anything, because he does not know what he is saying.

> It is narrated in a sahih report from the Prophet (peace be upon him) that a man came to him and confessed to zina (fornication or adultery), and he said: "Has he been drinking wine?" A man got up and smelt his mouth, and did not detect any smell of wine. Narrated by Muslim (1695).

This indicates that if he had drunk wine, then his confession would not be acceptable. By the same token, divorce issued by someone in this state does not count as such.

Imam al-Bukhari (may Allah have mercy on him) said:

'Uthmaan said: The one who is insane or drunk cannot issue a divorce. Ibn 'Abbas said: Divorce issued by one who is drunk or one who is compelled does not count as such.

Ibn al-Mundhir (may Allah have mercy on him) said: This is proven from 'Uthmaan, and we do not know of anyone among the Sahaabah who disagreed with him.

Majallat al-Buhooth al-Islamiyyah, 32/252; al-Mawsoo'ah al-Fiqhiyyah, 29/18; al-Insaaf, 8/433

All four Sunni schools of Islamic jurisprudence are quite similar and provide a wide range of solutions for different issues of Islamic Shariah, but the question arises are the four schools divine? So, the answer is No, divine is the Quran and the Prophet who read it to the people. No person other than the Prophet Muhammad (peace be upon him) can be called infallible in the realm of Islam telling. All other men are bound to the Quran and Sunnah to interpret Islam.

CHAPTER IV

A Worldly View of Talaq

Laws of Arab States

(i) **Algeria:** Is a theocratic State, which declares Islam to be its official religion. Muslims of the Sunni sect constitute its majority. On the issue in hand, it has enacted the following legislation: Code of Family Law 1984 Law No.84-11 of 1984 as amended in 2005 "Article 49. Divorce cannot be established except by a judgment of the court, preceded by an attempt at reconciliation for a period not exceeding three months."

(ii) **Egypt:** Is a secular State. Muslims of the Sunni sect constitute its majority. On the issue in hand, it has enacted the following legislation: Law of Personal Status 1929 Law 25 of 1929 as amended by Law 100 of 1985 "Article 1. A Talaq pronounced under the effect of intoxication or compulsion shall not be effective. Article 2. A conditional Talaq which is not meant to take effect immediately shall have no effect if it is used as an inducement to do some act or to abstain from it. Article 3. A Talaq accompanied by a number, expressly or impliedly, shall not be effective except as a single revocable divorce. Article 4. Symbolic expressions of talaq, i.e., words which may or may not bear the implication of a divorce, shall not affect a divorce unless the husband actually intended it."

(iii) **Iraq:** Is a theocratic State, which declares Islam to be its official religion. The majority of Iraq's Muslims is Shia. On the issue in hand, it has enacted the following legislation: Code of Personal Status 1959 Law 188 of 1959 as amended by Law 90 of 1987 "Article 35. No divorce shall be effective when pronounced by the persons mentioned below: (a) one who is intoxicated, insane or imbecile, under duress, or not in his senses due to anger, sudden calamity, old age or sickness; (b) a person in death-sickness or in a condition which in all probabilities is fatal and of which he actually dies, survived by his wife." Article 37. (1) Where a Talaq is coupled with a number, express or implied, not more than one divorce shall take place. (2) If a woman is divorced thrice on three separate occasions by her husband, no revocation or remarriage would be permissible after that. Article 39. (1) When a person intends to divorce his wife, he shall institute a suit in the Court of Personal Status requesting that it be affected and that an order be issued therefor. If a person cannot so approach the court, registration of the divorce in the court during the period of Iddat shall be binding on him. (2) The certificate of marriage shall remain valid till it is cancelled by the court."

(iv) **Jordan:** Is a secular State. Muslims of the Sunni sect constitute its majority. On the issue in hand, it has enacted the following legislation: Code of Personal Status 1976 Law 61 of 1976 "Article 88. (1) Talaq shall not be effective if pronounced under intoxication, bewilderment, compulsion, mental disorder, depression or effect of sleep. (2) 'Bewildered' is one who has lost senses due to anger or provocation, etc., and cannot understand what he is saying. Article 90. A divorce coupled with a number, expressly or impliedly, as also a divorce repeated in the same sitting, will not take effect except as a single divorce. Article 94. Every divorce shall be revocable except the final third, one before consummation and one with consideration. Article 98. Where an irrevocable Talaq was pronounced once or twice, renewal of marriage with the consent of parties is not prohibited."

v) **Kuwait:** Is a theocratic State, which declares Islam to be the official religion. Muslims of the Sunni sect constitute its majority.

On the issue in hand, it has the following legislation in place: Code of Personal Status 1984 Law 51 of 1984 "Article 102. Talaq may be affected by major and sane men acting by their free will and understanding the implications of their action. Therefore, Talaq shall not take effect if the husband is mentally handicapped, imbecile, under coercion, mistake, intoxication, fear or high anger affecting his speech and action. Article 109. If a Talaq is pronounced with a number (two, three) by words, signs or writing, only one Talaq shall take effect."

(vi) **Lebanon:** Is a secular State. Muslims constitute its majority, which is estimated to be 54% (27% Shia, and 27% Sunni). On the issue in hand, it has enacted the following legislation: Family Rights Law 1962 Law of 16 July 1962 "Article 104. A divorce by a drunk person shall have no effect. Article 105. A divorce pronounced under coercion shall have no effect."

(vii) **Libya:** Is a theocratic State, which declares Islam to be its official religion. Muslims of the Sunni sect constitute its majority. On the issue in hand, it has enacted the following legislation: Family Law 1984 Law 10 of 1984 as amended by Law 15 of 1984 "Article 28. Divorce is termination of the marriage bond. No divorce will become effective in any case except by a decree of a competent court and subject to the provision of Article 30. Article 29. Divorce is of two kinds – revocable and irrevocable. Revocable divorce does not terminate the marriage till the expiry of Iddat. Irrevocable divorce terminates the marriage forthwith. Article 30. All divorces shall be revocable except a third-time divorce, one before consummation of marriage, one for a consideration, and those specified in this law to be irrevocable. Article 31. A divorce shall be effective only if pronounced in clear words showing intention to dissolve the marriage. Symbolic or metaphorical expression will not dissolve the marriage. Article 32.

A divorce pronounced by a minor or insane person, or if pronounced under coercion, or with no clear intention to dissolve the marriage, shall have no legal effect. Article 33. (1) A divorce meant to be effect on some action or omission of the wife shall have no legal effect. (2) A divorce given with a view to binding the wife to an oath or restrain her from doing something shall have no legal effect. (3) A divorce to which a number is attached, by express words or a gesture, shall effect only a single revocable divorce, except when it is pronounced for the third time. Article 35. The marriage may be dissolved by mutual consent of the parties. Such a divorce must be registered with the court. If the parties cannot agree on the terms of such a divorce, they shall approach the 37 court, and it will appoint arbitrators to settle the matter or reconcile them. Article 47. A divorce must be pronounced in a court and in the presence of the other party or his or her representative. The court shall before giving effect to a divorce exhaust all possibilities of reconciliation."

viii) **Morocco:** Is a theocratic State, which declares Islam to be its official religion. Muslims of the Sunni sect constitute its majority. On the issue in hand, it has enacted the following legislation: Code of Personal Status 2004 Law 70.03 of 2004 "Article 79. Whoever divorces his wife by Talaq must petition the court for permission to register it with the Public Notaries of the area where the matrimonial home is situate, or where the wife resides, or where the marriage took place. Article 80. The petition will mention the identity of spouses, their professions, addresses, number of children, if any, with their age, health condition and educational status. It must be supported by a copy of the marriage agreement and a document stating the husband's social status and financial obligations. Article 81. The court shall summon the spouses and attempt reconciliation. If the husband deliberately abstains, this will be deemed to be withdrawal of the petition. If the wife abstains, the court will notify her that if she does not present herself the petition may be decided in her absence. If the husband has fraudulently given a wrong address for the wife, he may be prosecuted at her instance. Article 82. The court will hear the parties and their witnesses in camera and take all possible steps to reconcile them, including appointment of arbitrators or a family reconciliation council, and if there are children such efforts shall be exhausted within thirty days. If reconciliation takes place, a report will be filed with the court. Article 83. If reconciliation attempts fail, the court shall fix an amount to be deposited by the husband in the court within thirty days towards payment of the wife's post-divorce dues and maintenance of children.

Article 90. No divorce is permissible for a person who is not in his senses or is under coercion or provocation. Article 92. Multiple expressions of divorce, oral or written, shall have the effect of a single divorce only. Article 123. Every divorce pronounced by the husband shall be revocable, except a third-time divorce, divorce before consummation of 38 marriage, divorce by mutual consent, and divorce by Khula or Talaq-e Tafweez.

(ix) **Sudan:** Is a theocratic State, which declares Islam to be its official religion. Muslims of the Sunni sect constitute its majority. On the issue in hand, it has the following legislation in place: Law on Talaq 1935 Judicial Proclamation No.4 of 1935 "Article 1. A divorce uttered in a state of intoxication or under duress shall be invalid and ineffective. Article 2. A contingent divorce which is not meant to be effective immediately and is used as an inducement or threat shall have not effect. Article 3. A formula of divorce coupled with a number, expressly or impliedly, shall effect only one divorce. Article 4. Metaphorical expressions used for a divorce shall have the effect of dissolving the marriage only if the husband actually meant a divorce."

(x) **Syria:** Is a secular State. Muslims of the Sunni sect constitute its majority. On the issue in hand, it has enacted the following legislation: Code of Personal Status 1953 Law 59 of 1953 as amended by Law 34 of 1975 "Article 89. No divorce shall take place when the man is drunk, out of his senses, or under duress. A person is out of his senses when due to anger, etc. he does not appreciate what he says. Article 90. A conditional divorce shall have no effect if not actually intended and used only as an inducement to do or abstain from doing something or as an oath or persuasion. Article 92. If a divorce is coupled with a number, expressly or impliedly, not more than one divorce shall take place. Article 94. Every divorce shall be revocable except a third-time divorce, one before consummation, a divorce with a consideration, and a divorce stated in this Code to be irrevocable.

Article 117. Where a person divorces his wife the court may, if satisfied that he has arbitrarily done so without any reasonable cause and that as a result of the divorce the wife shall suffer damage and become destitute, give a decision, with due regard to the husband's financial condition and the amount of wife's suffering, that he should pay her compensation not exceeding three years' maintenance, in addition to maintenance payable 39 during the period of Iddat. It may be directed to be paid either in a lump sum or in instalments as the circumstances of a case may require.

xi) **Tunisia:** Is a theocratic State, which declares Islam to be its official religion. Muslims of the Sunni sect constitute its majority. On the issue in hand, it has enacted the following legislation: Code of Personal Status 1956 Law 13-8 of 1956 as amended by Law 7 of 1981 "Article 31.(1) A decree of divorce shall be given: (i) with the mutual consent of the parties; or (ii) at the instance of either party on the ground of injury; or (iii) if the husband insists on divorce or the wife demands it. The party causing material or mental injury by the fact of divorce under clauses (ii) and (iii) shall be directed to indemnify the aggrieved spouse. (2) As regards the woman to be indemnified for material injury in terms of money, the same shall be paid to her after the expiry of Iddat and may be in the form of retention of the matrimonial home. This indemnity will be subject to revision, increase or decrease in accordance with the changes in the circumstances of the divorced wife until she is alive or until she changes her marital status by marrying again. If the former husband dies, this indemnity will be a charge on his estate and will have to be met by his heirs if they consent to it and will be decided by the court if they disagree. They may pay her in a lump sum within one year from the former husband's death the indemnity claimable by her. Article 32 (1) No divorce shall be decreed except after the court has made an overall inquiry into the causes of rift and failed to effect reconciliation. (2) Where no reconciliation is possible the court shall provide, even if not asked to, for all important matters relating to the residence of the spouses, maintenance and custody of children and meeting the children, except when the parties specifically agree to forgo all or any of these rights. The court shall fix the maintenance on the basis of all those facts which it comes to know while attempting reconciliation. All important matters shall be provided for in the decree, which shall be Non appealable but can be reviewed for making additional provisions. (3) The court of first instance shall pass orders in the matters of divorce and all concerning matters including the compensation money to which the divorced wife may be entitled after the expiry of Iddat. The portions of the decree relating to custody, maintenance, compensation, residence and right to visit children shall be executed immediately."

(xii) **United Arab Emirates:** Is a theocratic State, as the Federal Constitution declares Islam to be the official religion. The

Constitution also provides for freedom of religion, in accordance with established customs. Muslims of Sunni sect constitute its majority. On the issue in hand, it has the following legislation in place: Law of Personal Status 2005 Federal Law No.28 of 2005 "Article 140(1). If a husband divorces his wife after consummation of a valid marriage by his unilateral action and without any move for divorce from her side, she will be entitled to compensation besides maintenance for Iddat. The amount of compensation will be decided with due regard to the means of the husband and the hardship suffered by the wife, but it shall not exceed the amount of one year's maintenance payable in law to a woman of her status. (2) The Kazi may decree the compensation, to be paid as a lump sum or in instalments, according to the husband's ability to pay."

(xiii) **Yemen:** Is a theocratic State, which declares Islam to be the official religion. Muslims of the Sunni sect constitute its majority. On the issue in hand, it has the following legislation in place: Decree on Personal Status 1992 Decree 20 of 1992 "Article 61. A divorce shall not be effective if pronounced by a man who is drunk, or has lost his senses, or has no power of discernment, if this is shown by his condition and action. Article 64. A divorce to which a number is attached, whatever be the number, will effect only a single revocable divorce. Article 65. The words saying that if the wife did or failed to do something she will stand divorced will not effect a divorce. Article 66. The words that if an oath or vow is broken it will effect a divorce will not dissolve the marriage even if the said oath or vow is broken. Article 67. A divorce can be revoked by the husband during the Iddat period. After the expiry of Iddat, a direct remarriage between them will be lawful. Article 71. If a man arbitrarily divorces his wife without any reasonable ground and it causes hardship to her, the court may grant her compensation payable by the husband not exceeding maintenance for one year in accordance with her status. The court may decide if the compensation will be paid as a lump sum or in instalments."

Laws of Southeast Asian States

(i) **Indonesia**: The Constitution of Indonesia guarantees freedom of religion among Indonesians. However, the Government recognizes only six official religions – Islam, Protestantism, Catholicism, Hinduism, Buddhism, and Confucianism. Muslims of the Sunni sect constitute its majority. On the issue in hand, it has the following legislation in place: (a) Law of Marriage 1974 Law 1 of 1974 "Article 38. A divorce shall be effected only in the court and the court shall not permit a divorce before attempting reconciliation between the parties. Divorce shall be permissible only for sufficient reasons indicating breakdown of marriage. Article 41. In the event of a divorce both the parents shall continue to be responsible for the maintenance of their children. As regards custody of children, in case of a dispute between them the court shall take a decision. Expenses of maintenance and education shall be primarily the father's liability, but if he is unable to discharge this liability the court may transfer it to the mother. The court may also direct the former husband to pay alimony to the divorced wife." (b) Marriage Regulations 1975 Regulation 9 of 1975 "Article 14. A man married under Islamic law wanting to divorce his wife shall by a letter notify his intention to the District Court seeking proceedings for that purpose. Article 15. On receiving a letter the court shall, within thirty days, summon the parties and gather from them all relevant facts. Article 16. If the court is satisfied of the existence of any of the grounds mentioned in Article 19 below and is convinced that no reconciliation between the parties is possible it will allow a divorce. Article 17. Immediately after allowing a divorce as laid down in Article 16 above the court shall issue a certificate of divorce and send it to the Registrar for registration of the divorce.

Article 19. A divorce may be allowed on the petition of either party if the other party: (a) has committed adultery or become addict to alcohol, drugs, gambling or another serious vice; (b) has deserted the aggrieved party for two years or more without any legal ground and against the said party's will; (c) has been imprisoned for at least five years; (d) has treated the aggrieved party with cruelty of an injurious nature; 42 (e) has been suffering from a physical deformity affecting conjugal duties, or where relations between the spouses have become too much strained making reconciliation impossible."

(ii) **Malaysia:** Under the Constitution of Malaysia, Islam is the official religion of the country, but other religions are permitted to be practiced in peace and harmony. Muslims of the Sunni sect constitute its majority. On the issue in hand, it has the following legislation in place: Islamic Family Law Act 1984 Act 304 of 1984 "Article 47. (1) A husband or a wife who desires a divorce shall present an application for divorce to the court in the prescribed form accompanied by a statutory declaration containing (a) particulars of the marriage and the name, ages and sex of the children, if any, of the marriage; (b) particulars of the facts giving the court jurisdiction under Section 45; (c) particulars of any previous matrimonial proceedings between the parties, including the place of the proceedings; (d) a statement as to the reasons for desiring divorce; (e) a statement as to whether any, and if so, what steps have been taken to effect reconciliation; (f) the terms of any agreement regarding maintenance and habitation of the wife and the children of the marriage, if any, and the division of any assets acquired through the joint effort of the parties, if any, or where no such agreement has been reached, the applicant's proposals regarding those matters; and (g) particulars of the order sought. (2) Upon receiving an application for divorce, the court shall cause summons to be served on the other party together with a copy of the application and the statutory declaration made by the applicant, and the summons shall direct the other party to appear before the court so as to enable it to inquire whether or not the other party consents to the divorce. (3) If the other party consents to the divorce and the court is satisfied after due inquiry and investigation that the marriage has irretrievably broken down, the court shall advise the husband to pronounce one Talaq before the court. (4) The court shall record the fact of the pronouncement of one Talaq and shall send a certified copy of the record to the appropriate Registrar and to the Chief Registrar for registration. (5) Where the other party does not consent to the divorce or it appears to the court that there is reasonable possibility of a reconciliation between the parties, the court shall as soon as possible appoint a Conciliatory Committee consisting of a religious officer as Chairman and two other persons, one to act for the husband and the other for the wife, and refer the case to the Committee.

(6) In appointing the two persons under sub-section (5) the court shall, where possible, give preference to close relatives of the parties having knowledge of the circumstances of the case. (7) The court may give directions to the Conciliatory Committee as to the conduct of the conciliation and it shall conduct it in accordance with such directions. (8) If the Committee is unable to agree or if the court is not satisfied with its conduct of the conciliation, the court may remove the Committee and appoint another Committee in its place. (9) The Committee shall endeavor to effect reconciliation within a period of six months from the date of its being constituted or such further period as may be allowed by the court. (10) The Committee shall require the attendance of the

parties and shall give each of them an opportunity of being heard and may hear such other persons and make such inquiries as it thinks fit and may, if it considers it necessary, adjourn its proceedings from time to time. (11) If the Conciliatory Committee is unable to effect reconciliation and is unable to persuade the parties to resume their conjugal relationship, it shall issue a certificate to that effect and may append to the certificate such recommendations as it thinks fit regarding maintenance and custody of the minor children of the marriage, if any, regarding division of property and other matters related to the marriage. (12) No advocate and solicitor shall appear or act for any party in any proceeding before a Conciliatory Committee and no party shall be represented by any person other than a member of his or her family without the leave of the Conciliatory Committee. (13) Where the Committee reports to the court that reconciliation has been effected and the parties have resumed their conjugal relationship, the court shall dismiss the application for divorce. (14) Where the Committee submits to the court a certificate that it is unable to effect reconciliation and to persuade the parties to resume the conjugal relationship, the court shall advise the husband to pronounce one Talaq before the court, and where the court is unable to procure the presence of the husband before the court to pronounce one Talaq, or where the husband refuses to pronounce one Talaq, the court shall refer the case to the Hakams [arbitrators] for action according to section 48. (15) The requirement of sub-section (5) as to reference to a Conciliatory Committee shall not apply in any case (a) where the applicant alleges that he or she has been deserted by an does not know the whereabouts of the other party; (b) where the other party is residing outside West Malaysia and it is unlikely that he or she will be within the jurisdiction of the court within six months after the date of the application; (c) where the other party is imprisoned for a term of three years or more; (d) where the applicant alleges that the other party is suffering from incurable mental illness; or (e) where the court is satisfied that there are exceptional circumstances which make reference to a Conciliatory Committee impracticable. (16) Save as provided in sub-section (17), a Talaq pronounced by the husband or an order made by the court shall not be effective until the expiry of the Iddat. (17) If the wife is pregnant at the time the Talaq is pronounced or the order is made, the Talaq or the order shall not be effective until the pregnancy ends."

(iii) **Philippines:** Is a secular State. Christians constitute its majority. On the issue in hand, it has the following legislation in place: Code of Muslim Personal Law 1977 Decree No.1083 of 1977 "Article 46. (1) A divorce by Talaq may be effected by the husband in a single repudiation of his wife during her Tuhr [non-menstrual period] within which he has totally abstained from carnal relations with her. (2) Any number of repudiations made during one Tuhr [non-menstrual period] shall constitute only one repudiation and shall become irrevocable after the expiration of the prescribed Iddat. (3) A husband who repudiates his wife, either for the first or second time, shall have the right to take her back within the Iddat period by resumption of cohabitation without need of a new contract of marriage. Should he fail to do so, the repudiation shall become irrevocable. Article 85. Within seven days after the revocation of a divorce the husband shall, with the wife's consent, send a statement thereof to the Circuit Registrar in whose records the divorce was previously entered. Article 161. (1) A Muslim male who has pronounced a Talaq shall, without delay, file with the Clerk of the Sharia Circuit Court of the place where his family resides a written notice of such fact and the circumstances attending thereto, after having served a copy to the wife concerned. The Talaq pronounced shall not become irrevocable until after the expiration of the prescribed Iddat. (2) Within seven days from receipt of notice the Clerk of the Court shall require each of the parties to nominate a representative. The representatives shall be appointed by the court to constitute, with the Clerk of the Court as Chairman, an Agama [religious scholars] Arbitration Council which shall try and submit to the court a report on the result of arbitration on the basis of which, and such other evidence as may be allowed, the court will pass an order. (3) The provisions of this Article will be observed if the wife exercises right to Talaq-e-Tafweez.

Article 183. A person who fails to comply with the requirements of Article 85, 161 and 162 of this Code shall be penalized by imprisonment or a fine of two hundred to two thousand Pesos, or both."

Laws of Sub-continental States

(i) **Pakistan & Bangladesh:** Are both theocratic States, wherein Islam is the official religion. In both countries Muslims of the Sunni sect constitute the majority. On the issue in hand, it has the following legislation in place: Muslim Family Laws Ordinance 1961 Ordinance VIII of 1961 amended in Bangladesh by Ordinance 114 of 1985 (Bangladesh changes noted below relevant provisions) "Section 7. (1) Any man who wishes to divorce his wife shall, as soon as may be after the pronouncement of Talaq in any form whatsoever, give the Chairman a notice in writing of his having done so, and shall supply a copy thereof to the wife. (2) Whoever contravenes the provision of sub-section (1) shall be punishable with simple imprisonment for a term which may extend to one year, or with fine which may extend to five thousand rupees, or with both. [Bangladesh: ten thousand takas] (3) Save as provided in sub-section (5), a Talaq unless revoked earlier, expressly or otherwise, shall not be effective until the expiration of ninety days from the day on which notice under subsection (1) is delivered to the Chairman. (4) Within thirty days of the receipt of notice under sub-section (1) the Chairman shall constitute an Arbitration Council for the purpose of bringing about reconciliation between the parties, and the Arbitration council shall take all steps necessary to bring about such reconciliation. (5) If the wife be pregnant at the time Talaq is pronounced, Talaq shall not be effective until the period mentioned in sub-section (3) or of pregnancy, whichever is later, ends. (6) Nothing shall debar a wife whose marriage has been terminated by Talaq effective under this section from re-marrying the same husband without any intervening marriage with a third person, unless such termination is for the third time so effective."

(ii) **Sri Lanka:** Is a secular State. Buddhists constitute its majority. On the issue in hand, it has the following legislation in place: Muslim Marriage and Divorce Act 1951 Act 6 of 1951 as amended by Act 40 of 2006 46 "Section 17 (4) Save as otherwise hereinafter expressly provided, every marriage contracted between Muslims after the commencement of this Act shall be registered, as hereinafter provided, immediately upon the conclusion of the Nikah ceremony connected therewith. (5) In the case of each such marriage, the duty of causing it to be registered is hereby imposed upon the following persons concerned in the marriage; (a) the bridegroom, (b) the guardian of the bride, and (c) the person who conducted the Nikah ceremony connected with the marriage. Section 27. Where a husband desires to divorce his wife, the procedure laid down in Schedule II shall be followed." (2) Where a wife desires to effect a divorce from her husband on any ground not referred to in sub-section (1), being a divorce of any description permitted to a wife by the Muslim law governing the sect to which the parties belong, the procedure laid down in the Schedule III shall be followed so far as the nature of the divorce claimed in each case renders it possible or necessary to follow that procedure. 29. 'Talaq-e-biddat' is effective, the very moment it is pronounced. It is irrevocable when it is pronounced.

The world recognizes multiple pronouncement of talaq at a time as one but despite this international recognition many of our learned scholars put their endless efforts to prove the triple talaq a part of Islamic teaching though it has nothing to do with Islam.

CHAPTER V

Indian Supreme Court and Triple Talaq

Sayara Bano, the petitioner, had approached the Supreme Court of India challenging the divorce pronounced by her husband, Rizwan Ahmad, on 10 October 2015. In the presence of two witnesses, namely Mohammed Yaseen (son of Abdul Majeed) and Ayaaz Ahmad (son of Ityaz Hussain), Rizwan Ahmad declared, "I gave talaq, talaq, talaq, hence like this I divorce from you from my wife. From this date there is no relation of husband and wife. From today I am haram, and I have become na-mehram. In future you are free for using your life."

The petitioner sought a declaration that the 'talaq-e-biddat' (instant triple talaq) pronounced by her husband be declared void ab initio. She contended that such a form of divorce, which abruptly, unilaterally, and irrevocably dissolved the marital relationship—purportedly under Section 2 of the Muslim Personal Law (Shariat) Application Act, 1937 (hereinafter referred to as the Shariat Act)—should be held unconstitutional. During the course of the hearing, it was submitted on behalf of the petitioner that the practice of 'talaq-e-biddat' was not an integral part of Shariat (Muslim personal law). It was further argued that such a form of divorce could not be considered a "rule of decision" under the Shariat Act. The petitioner also asserted that the practice of 'talaq-e-biddat' violated fundamental rights guaranteed under Articles 14, 15, and 21 of the Constitution of India. Additionally, she maintained that the practice could not be protected under the religious freedoms and cultural rights granted to religious denominations or their sections under Articles 25(1), 26(b), and 29 of the Constitution.

The Supreme Court of India mentioned in its judgment (Para. 11 and 12) the practiced modes of 'talaq' amongst Muslims:

> Since the issue under consideration is the dissolution of marriage by 'talaq', under the Islamic law of divorce, it is imperative, to understand the concept of 'talaq'. In this behalf, it is relevant to mention, that under the Islamic law, divorce is classified into three categories. Talaq understood simply, is a means of divorce, at the instance of the husband. 'Khula', is another mode of divorce, this divorce is at the instance of the wife. The third category of divorce is 'mubaraat' – divorce by mutual consent. 12. 'Talaq', namely, divorce at the instance of the husband, is also of three kinds – 'talaq-e-ahsan', 'talaq-e-hasan' and 'talaq-e-biddat'. The petitioner's contention before this Court is, that 'talaq-e-ahsan', and 'talaqe-hasan' are both approved by the 'Quran' and 'hadith'. 'Talaq-e-ahsan', is considered as the 'most reasonable' form of divorce, whereas 'talaq-ehasan' is also considered as 'reasonable'. It was submitted, that 'talaq-e-biddat' is neither recognized by the 'Quran' nor by 'hadith', and as such, is to be considered as sacrosanct to Muslim religion. The controversy which has arisen for consideration before this Court, is with reference to 'talaq-e-biddat'.

Para. 13 (Supreme Court's judgment on the unconstitutionality of Triple Talaq 2017)

> It is necessary for the determination of the present controversy, to understand the parameters, and the nature of the different kinds of 'talaq'. 'Talaq-e-ahsan' is a single pronouncement of 'talaq' by the husband, followed by a period of abstinence. The period of abstinence is described as 'iddat'. The

duration of the 'iddat' is ninety days or three menstrual cycles (in case, where the wife is menstruating). Alternatively, the period of 'iddat' is of three lunar months (in case, the wife is not menstruating). If the couple resumes cohabitation or intimacy, within the period of 'iddat', the pronouncement of divorce is treated as having been revoked. Therefore, 'talaq-e-ahsan' is revocable. Conversely, if there is no resumption of cohabitation or intimacy, during the period of 'iddat', then the divorce becomes final and irrevocable, after the expiry of the 'iddat' period. It is considered irrevocable because, the couple is forbidden to resume marital relationship thereafter, unless they contract a fresh 'nikah' (-marriage), with a fresh 'mahr'. 'Mahr' is a mandatory payment, in the form of money or possessions, paid or promised to be paid, by the groom or by the groom's father, to the bride, at the time of marriage, which legally becomes her property. However, on the third pronouncement of such a 'talaq', the couple cannot remarry, unless the wife first marries someone else, and only after her marriage with other person has been dissolved (either through 'talaq' - divorce, or death), can the couple remarry. Amongst Muslims, 'talaq-e-ahsan' is regarded as – 'the most proper' form of divorce.

Para. 14 (Supreme Court's judgment on the unconstitutionality of Triple Talaq 2017)

'Talaq-e-hasan' is pronounced in the same manner, as 'talaq-eahsan'. Herein, in place of a single pronouncement, there are three successive pronouncements. After the first pronouncement of divorce, if there is resumption of cohabitation within a period of one month, the pronouncement of divorce is treated as having been revoked. The same procedure is mandated to be followed, after the expiry of the first month (during which marital ties have not been resumed). 'Talaq' is pronounced again. After the second pronouncement of 'talaq', if there is resumption of cohabitation within a period of one month, the pronouncement of divorce is treated as having been revoked. It is significant to note, that the first and the second pronouncements may be revoked by the husband. If he does so, either expressly or by resuming conjugal relations, 'talaq' pronounced by the husband becomes ineffective, as if no 'talaq' had ever been expressed. If the third 'talaq' is pronounced, it becomes irrevocable. Therefore, if no revocation is made after the first and the second declaration, and the husband makes the third pronouncement, in the third 'tuhr' (period of purity), as soon as the third declaration is made, the 'talaq' becomes irrevocable, and the marriage stands dissolved, whereafter, the wife has to observe the required 'iddat' (the period after divorce, during which a woman cannot remarry. Its purpose is to ensure, that the male parent of any offspring is clearly identified). And after the third 'iddat', the husband and wife cannot remarry, unless the wife first marries someone else, and only after her marriage with another person has been dissolved (either through divorce or death), can the couple remarry. The distinction between 'talaq-eashan' and 'talaq-e-hasan' is, that in the former there is a single pronouncement of 'talaq' followed by abstinence during the period of 'iddat', whereas, in the latter there are three pronouncements of 'talaq', interspersed with abstinence. As against 'talaq-e-ahsan', which is regarded as 'the most proper' form of divorce, Muslims regard 'talaq-e-hasan' only as 'the proper form of divorce'.

Para. 15 (Supreme Court's judgment on the unconstitutionality of Triple Talaq 2017)

> The third kind of 'talaq' is – 'talaq-e-biddat'. This is effected by one definitive pronouncement of 'talaq' such as, "I talaq you irrevocably" or three simultaneous pronouncements, like "talaq, talaq, talaq", uttered at the same time, simultaneously. In 'talaq-e-biddat', divorce is effective forthwith. The instant talaq, unlike the other two categories of 'talaq' is irrevocable at the very moment it is pronounced. Even amongst Muslims 'talaq-e-biddat', is considered irregular.

Para.16 (Supreme Court's judgment on the unconstitutionality of Triple Talaq 2017)

> According to the petitioner, there is no mention of 'talaq-e-biddat' in the Quran. It was however acknowledged, that the practice of 'talaq-ebiddat' can be traced to the second century, after the advent of Islam. It was submitted, that 'talaq-e-biddat' is recognized only by a few Sunni schools. Most prominently, by the Hanafi sect of Sunni Muslims. It was however emphasized, that even those schools that recognized 'talaq-ebiddat' described it, "as a sinful form of divorce". It is acknowledged, that this form of divorce, has been described as "bad in theology, but good in law". We have recorded the instant position at this juncture, because learned counsel for the rival parties, uniformly acknowledge the same.

Para.90 (Supreme Court's judgment on the unconstitutionality of Triple Talaq 2017)

The Supreme Court highlighted, that Imam Abu Hanifa did not himself record his own understanding what the Prophet Muhammad had said. It was pointed out, that he had two disciples – Abu Yusuf and Imam Mohammed. It was submitted, that Imam Abu Yusuf in his book "Ikhtilaaf Abi Hanifah wabni Abi Laila" (first edition, 1357) stated the following on the triple talaq:

> "i. If the man said to his wife, "Your matter is in your hand, she said, "I have divorced myself three times". Abu Haneefah (may Allah be pleased with him) says: "If the husband intends three times, then it is three."

References were also made to the writings of Imam Abu Mohammed in his book entitled "Al-Mautta" (first volume), wherein he asserted as under:

> "i. Muhammad says: So we follow this that if she chooses her husband then it will not be counted a divorce, and if she chooses herself then it is according to what her husband intended, if his intention is one hen it will be counted one irrevocable (Baainah) divorce, and if his is three it will be three divorces. This is the saying of Abu Hanifah."

References given by the Supreme Court about Triple Talaq:

Para.91 (Supreme Court's judgment on the unconstitutionality of Triple Talaq 2017)

"(i) Most of the Ulema take the innovative divorce as effective (Baday alsanay, fasl Hukum Talaq-al Bidaa, Kitab al-Talaq, 3/153).

(ii) What do you think about the effectiveness of pronouncing divorce thrice upon one's pregnant wife either in one go or in three different sessions, Imam Malik replied in the affirmative. (AI-Mudawwana, 2/68)

(iii) The validity of triple talaq is also endorsed by all Ahl Al Sunnah jurists. Allama Ibn Quda ma adds that: "This view is attributed to Abdul/ah ibn Abbas. The same stance is shared by most of the successors and later scholars." (AI-Mughni Ii Ibn Qudama, 10/334)

(iv) The Book, Sunnah, and the consensus view of classical authorities is that Triple Talaq is effective, even if pronounced in one go. The act in itself is, however, a sin." (Ahkam al-Quran Iil Jassas, 2/85)

(v) Imam Shafi'i (of Shafi'i School) has stated as follows in his book entitled as Al-Umm (fifth volume): If he says you are divorced absolutely, with the intention of triple divorce then it will be considered triple divorce and if he intends one it will be considered one divorce and if he says you are divorced with the intention of three it will be considered three. (page 359)

(vi) Mauffaqud Din Abi Muhammed Abdillah Ben Ahmed Ben Muhammed Ben Qudamah Al-Muqaddasi Al-Jammaili Al-Dimashqi AlSalihi Al-Hanbali (of the Hanbali School) in his book entitled as AlMughni (tenth volume) has stated as follows: Ahmed said: If he says to wife: Divorce yourself, intending three, and she has divorced herself thrice, it will be considered three, and if he has intended one then it will considered one. (page 394)

(vii) Allama Ibn Qudama, a Hanbali jurist is of the view that if one divorces thrice with a single utterance, this divorce will be effective and she will be unlawful for him until she marries someone else. Consummation of marriage is immaterial. The validity of Triple Talaq is also endorsed by all Ahl Al Sunnah jurists. Allama Ibn Qudamma adds that: "This view is attributed to

Abdullah ibn Abbas, Abu Huraira, Umar, Abdullah ibn Umar, Abdullah ibn Amr ibn Aas, Abdullah ibn Masud, and 139 Anas. The same stance is shared by most of the successors and later scholars."" (Al-Mughni li Ibn Qudama, 10,334)".

Affidavit filed by All India Muslim Personal Board.

In the affidavit the submissions of the secretary of AIMPB are following:

"1. I am the Secretary of All India Muslim Personal Law Board which has been arraigned as Respondent No.3 and as Respondent No.8 respectively to the above-captioned Writ Petitions. I am conversant with the facts and circumstances of the present case, and I am competent to swear this Affidavit.

2. I say and submit that the All-India Muslim Personal Law Board will issue an advisory through its Website, Publications and Social Media Platforms and thereby advise the persons who perform 'Nikah' (marriage) and request them to do the following: -

(a) At the time of performing 'Nikah' (Marriage), the person performing the 'Nikah' will advise the Bridegroom/Man that in case of differences leading to Talaq the Bridegroom/Man shall not pronounce three divorces in one sitting since it is an undesirable practice in Shariat;

(b) That at the time of performing 'Nikah' (Marriage), the person performing the 'Nikah' will advise both the Bridegroom/Man and the Bride/Woman to incorporate a condition in the 'Nikahnama' to exclude resorting to pronouncement of three divorces by her husband in one sitting.

The Supreme Court of India also quoted in Para.6 of Judgment from the Asaf A.A. Fyzee's book Outlines of Muhammadan Law, 5th Edition, 2008 at page 10 that what Sharia is.

> "...What is morally beautiful that must be done; and what is morally ugly must not be done. That is law or Shariat and nothing else can be law. But what is absolutely and indubitably beautiful, and what is absolutely and indubitably ugly? These are the important legal questions; and who can answer them? Certainly not man, say the Muslim legists. We have the Qur'an which is the very word of God. Supplementary to it we have Hadith which are the Traditions of the Prophet- the records of his actions and his sayings- from which we must derive help and inspiration in arriving at legal decisions. If there is nothing either in the Qur'an or in the Hadith to answer the particular question which is before us, we have to follow the dictates of secular reason in accordance with certain definite principles. These principles constitute the basis of sacred law or Shariat as the Muslim doctors understand it. And it is these fundamental juristic notions which we must try to study and analyse before we approach the study of the Islamic civil law as a whole, or even that small part of it which in India is known as Muslim law."

The Supreme Court of India after a thoughtful consideration invalidated the practice of Triple Talaq and made it a punishable offence. The Supreme Court held the following declaration **Para. 191:**

The whole nation seems to be up in arms. There is seemingly an overwhelming majority of Muslim-women, demanding that the practice of 265 'talaq-e-biddat' which is sinful in theology, be declared as impermissible in law. The Union of India has also participated in the debate. It has adopted an aggressive posture, seeking the invalidation of the practice by canvassing, that it violates the fundamental rights enshrined in Part III of the Constitution, and by further asserting, that it even violates constitutional morality. During the course of hearing, the issue was hotly canvassed in the media. Most of the views expressed in erudite articles on the subject, hugely affirmed that the practice was demeaning. Interestingly even during the course of hearing, learned counsel appearing for the rival parties, were in agreement, and described the practice of 'talaq-e-biddat' differently as, unpleasant, distasteful and unsavory. The position adopted by others was harsher, they considered it as disgusting, loathsome and obnoxious. Some even described it as being debased, abhorrent and wretched.

Para.192

We have arrived at the conclusion, that 'talaq-e-biddat', is a matter of 'personal law' of Sunni Muslims, belonging to the Hanafi school. It constitutes a matter of their faith. It has been practiced by them, for at least 1400 years. We have examined whether the practice satisfies the constraints provided for under Article 25 of the Constitution, and have arrived at the conclusion, that it does not breach any of them. We have also come to the conclusion, that the practice being a component of 'personal law', has the protection of Article 25 of the Constitution.

Para.193

Religion is a matter of faith, and not of logic. It is not open to a court to accept an egalitarian approach, over a practice which constitutes an integral part of religion. The Constitution allows the followers of every religion, to follow their beliefs and religious traditions. The Constitution assures believers of all faiths, that their way of life, is guaranteed, and would not be subjected to any challenge, even though they may seem to others (-and even rationalists, practicing the same faith) unacceptable, in today's world and age. The Constitution extends this guarantee, because faith constitutes the religious consciousness, of the followers. It is this religious consciousness, which binds believers into separate entities. The Constitution endeavors to protect and preserve, the beliefs of each of the separate entities, under Article 25.

Para.194

Despite the views expressed by those who challenged the practice of 'talaq-e-biddat', being able to demonstrate that the practice transcends the barriers of constitutional morality (emerging from different provisions of the Constitution), we have found ourselves unable to persuade ourselves, from reaching out in support of the petitioner's concerns. We cannot accept the petitioners' claim, because the challenge raised is in respect of an issue of 'personal law' which has constitutional protection.

Para.195

In continuation of the position expressed above, we may acknowledge, that most of the prayers made to the Court (-at least on first blush) were persuasive enough, to solicit acceptance. Keeping in mind, that this opportunity had presented itself, so to say, to assuage the cause of Muslim women, it was felt, that the opportunity should not be lost. We are however satisfied that, that would not be the rightful course to tread. We were obliged to keep reminding ourselves, of the wisdom of the framers of the Constitution, who placed matters of faith in Part III of the Constitution. Therefore, any endeavor to proceed on issues canvassed before us would, tantamount to overlooking the clear letter of law. We cannot nullify and declare as unacceptable in law, what the Constitution decrees us, not only to protect, but also to enforce. The authority to safeguard and compel compliance, is vested under a special jurisdiction in constitutional Courts (-under Article 32, with the Supreme Court; and under Article 226, with the High Courts). Accepting the petitioners' prayers, would be in clear transgression of the constitutional mandate contained in Article 25.

Para.196

Such a call of conscience, as the petitioners desire us to accept, may well have a cascading effect. We say so, because the contention of the learned Attorney General was, that 'talaq-e-ahsan' and 'talaq-e-hasan' were also liable to be declared unconstitutional, for the same reasons as have been expressed with reference to 'talaq-e-biddat' (-for details, refer to paragraph 77 above). According to the learned Attorney General, the said forms of talaq also suffered from the same infirmities as 'talaq-e-biddat'. The practices of 'polygamy' and 'halala' amongst Muslims are already under challenge before us. It is not difficult to comprehend, what kind of challenges would be raised by rationalists, assailing practices of different faiths on diverse grounds, based on all kinds of enlightened sensibilities. We have to be guarded, lest we find our conscience traversing into every nook and corner of religious practices, and 'personal law'. Can a court, based on a righteous endeavor, declare that a matter of faith, be replaced – or be completely done away with. In the instant case, both prayers have been made. Replacement has been sought by reading the three pronouncements in 'talaq-e-biddat', as one. Alternatively, replacement has been sought by reading into 'talaq-e-biddat', measures of arbitration and conciliation, described in the Quran and the 'hadiths'. The prayer is also for setting aside the practice, by holding it to be unconstitutional. The wisdom emerging from judgments rendered by this Court is unambiguous, namely, that while examining issues falling in the realm of religious practices or 'personal law', it is not for a court to make a choice of something which it considers as forward looking or non-fundamentalist. It is not for a court to determine whether religious practices were prudent or progressive or regressive. Religion and 'personal law' must be perceived, as it is accepted, by the followers of the faith. And not, how another would like it to be (-including self-proclaimed rationalists, of the same faith). Article 25 obliges all Constitutional Courts to protect 'personal laws' and not to find fault therewith. Interference in matters of 'personal law' is clearly beyond judicial examination. The judiciary must, therefore, always exercise absolute restraint, no matter how compelling and attractive the opportunity to do societal good may seem. It is therefore, that this Court had the occasion to observe, "However laudable, desirable and attractive the result may seem ... an activist Court is not fully equipped to cope with the intricacies of the legislative subject and can at best advice and focus attention on the State polity on the problem and shake it from its slumber, goading it to awaken, march and reach the goal. For, in whatever measure be the concern of this Court, it compulsively needs to apply, motion, described in judicial parlance as self-restraint."

Para.197

We have arrived at the conclusion, that the legal challenge raised at the behest of the petitioners must fail, on the judicial front. Be that as it may, the question still remains, whether this is a fit case for us to exercise our jurisdiction under Article 142, "...for doing complete justice ...", in the matter. The reason for us to probe the possibility of exercising our jurisdiction under Article 142, arises only for one simple reason, that all concerned are unequivocal, that besides being arbitrary the practice of 'talaq-e-biddat' is gender discriminatory.

Para.198

A perusal of the consideration recorded by us reveals, that the practice of 'talaq-e-biddat' has been done away with, by way of legislation in a large number of egalitarian States, with sizeable Muslim population and even by theocratic Islamic States. Even the AIMPLB, the main contestant of the petitioners' prayers, whilst accepting the position canvassed on behalf of the petitioners, assumed the position, that it was not within the realm of judicial discretion, to set aside a matter of faith and religion. We have accepted the position assumed by the AIMPLB. It was however acknowledged even by the AIMPLB, that legislative will, could salvage the situation. This assertion was based on a conjoint reading of Articles 25(2) and Article 44 of the Constitution, read with entry 5 of the Concurrent List contained in the Seventh Schedule of the Constitution. There can be no doubt, and it is our definitive conclusion, that the position can only be salvaged by way of legislation. We understand that it is not appropriate to tender advice to the legislature, to enact law on an issue. However, the position as it presents in the present case, seems to be a little different. Herein, the views expressed by the rival parties are not in contradiction. The Union of India has appeared before us in support of the cause of the petitioners. The stance adopted by the Union of India is sufficient for us to assume, that the Union of India supports the petitioners' cause. Unfortunately, the Union seeks at our hands, what truly falls in its own. The main party that opposed the petitioner's' challenge, namely, the AIMPLB filed an affidavit before this Court affirming the following position: "1. I am the Secretary of All India Muslim Personal Board will issue an advisory through its Website, Publications and Social Media Platforms and thereby advise the persons who perform 'Nikah' (marriage) and request them to do the following:- (a) At the time of performing 'Nikah' (marriage), the person performing the 'Nikah' will advise the Bridegroom/Man that in case of differences leading to Talaq the Bridegroom/Man shall not pronounce three divorces in one sitting since it is an undesirable practice in Shariat; (b) That at the time of performing 'Nikah' (Marriage), the person performing the 'Nikah' will advise both the Bridegroom/Man and the Bride/Woman to incorporate a condition in the 'Nikahnama' to exclude resorting to pronouncement of three divorces by her husband in one sitting. 3. I say and submit that, in addition, the Board is placing on record, that the Working Committee of the Board had earlier already passed certain resolutions in the meeting held on 15th & 16th April 2017 in relation to Divorce (Talaq) in the Muslim community. Thereby it was resolved to convey a code of conduct/guidelines to be followed in the matters of divorce particularly emphasizing to avoid pronouncement of three divorces in one sitting. A copy of the resolution dated April 16, 2017, along with the relevant Translation of Resolution Nos. 2, 3, 4 & 5 relating to Talaq (Divorce) is enclosed herewith for the perusal of this Hon'ble Court and marked as Annexure A-1 (Colly) [Page Nos. 4 to 12] to the present Affidavit." A perusal of the above affidavit reveals, that the AIMPLB has undertaken to issue an advisory through its website, to advise those who enter into a matrimonial alliance, to agree in the 'nikah-nama', that their marriage would not be dissolvable by 'talaq-e-biddat'. The AIMPLB has sworn an affidavit to prescribe guidelines, to be followed in matters of divorce, emphasizing that 'talaq-e-biddat' be avoided. It would not be incorrect to assume, that even the AIMPLB is on board, to assuage the petitioner's cause.

Para.199

In view of the position expressed above, we are satisfied, that this is a case which presents a situation where this Court should exercise its discretion to issue appropriate directions under Article 142 of the Constitution. We therefore hereby direct, the Union of India to consider appropriate legislation, particularly with reference to ‘talaq-e-biddat’. We hope and expect, that the contemplated legislation will also take into consideration advances in Muslim ‘personal law’ – ‘Shariat’, as have been corrected by legislation the world over, even by theocratic Islamic States. When the British rulers in India provided succor to Muslims by legislation, and when remedial measures have been adopted by the Muslim world, we find no reason, for an independent India, to lag behind. Measures have been adopted for other religious denominations (see at IX – Reforms to ‘personal law’ in India), even in India, but not for the Muslims. We would therefore implore the legislature, to bestow its thoughtful consideration, to this issue of paramount importance. We would also beseech different political parties to keep their individual political gains apart, while considering the necessary measures requiring legislation.

Para.200

Till such time as legislation in the matter is considered, we are satisfied in injuncting Muslim husbands, from pronouncing ‘talaq-e-biddat’ as a means for severing their matrimonial relationship. The instant injunction, shall in the first instance, be operative for a period of six months. If the legislative process commences before the expiry of the period of six months, and a positive decision emerges towards redefining ‘talaq-ebiddat’ (three pronouncements of ‘talaq’, at one and the same time) – as one, or alternatively, if it is decided that the practice of ‘talaq-e-biddat’ be done away with altogether, the injunction would continue, till legislation is finally enacted. Failing which, the injunction shall cease to operate.

CHAPTER VI

The Outcome

The conclusions we arrive at after examining The Quran, The Hadith and The Fiqh have been mentioned in this chapter.

Person who is competent to pronounce Talaq:

1. A husband in a state of normality of mind, not being in a state of anger.
2. A husband who is not intoxicated or drunk.
3. A husband who is not under coercion or undue influence.
4. A husband who has minimum two witnesses present at the time of pronouncement.

Requisites after Talaq pronouncement:

1. The husband should keep the divorcee at his home without making relation with her so long as her iddah‘ ends.
2. The husband should provide all the basic needs till the divorcee completes her iddah’.
3. The husband if decides to apart the divorcee after the completion of her iddah‘ so he should pay her mehr if deferred and should also arrange, if possible, a farewell gift for her.
4. If the husband decides to keep her with good intention so they both may continue living as husband and wife.
5. The husband and divorcee should also reduce this divorce into writing for future references.
6. The husband has only two chances in lifetime to pronounce revocable divorces to his wife thereafter third pronouncement becomes final, and he should get apart

from his wife. The third pronouncement is meant to apart the wife from the husband as a moral punishment for the husband.

Common Misconceptions about Talaq in Muslim World:

Saying "Talaq" three times in one sitting equals to instant divorce.

Misconception: Uttering "Talaq, Talaq, Talaq" in one go means the marriage is immediately over.

Reality: Most scholars agree this is bid'ah (innovated) and not the recommended method. Proper procedure involves time and opportunities for reconciliation.

Talaq can be given in anger or joking.

Misconception: Even if said in anger or as a joke, it counts.

Reality: Anger that clouds judgment or extreme emotion makes pronouncement invalid.

Only the husband has the right to divorce.

Misconception: Women cannot initiate divorce.

Reality: Women can seek divorce through Khula or request conditions in the Nikah contract for Talaq-e-Tafweez (delegated divorce).

No need for waiting period (iddah)

Misconception: After divorce, the woman is free to remarry immediately.

Reality: Islam mandates a waiting period (iddah) of around 3 menstrual cycles to ensure no pregnancy and allow reconciliation.

Talaq by text or phone call is not valid

Misconception: Divorce must be in person.

Reality: If the words are clear and intentional, even text, email, or call can count, though not ideal.

Irrevocable after first Talaq.

Misconception: Once divorce is given, there's no turning back.

Reality: A couple can reconcile after the first or second Talaq during iddah without a new Nikah.

Women have no say in the process.

Misconception: Women are passive in the process.

Reality: Islam encourages fairness. Women can negotiate, seek arbitration, and appeal to courts.

Talaq must be in Arabic.

Misconception: If not said in Arabic, it's not valid.

Reality: Talaq in any language is valid if the intention is clear.

Triple Talaq is the only method

Misconception: Saying it three times is the Islamic way.

Reality: The Sunnah method is one Talaq, allowing for reflection and possible reconciliation. Saying Talaq three times or more was the tendency of Arabs. They used to repeat the words to emphasize the kalma.

Misconceptions about the Validity of Talaq.

- Talaq given in extreme anger is always valid.
- A mentally unstable person's talaq is valid.

- Talaq under intoxication counts.
- A sleeping person's talaq is valid.
- Talaq said in a dream is real.
- Talaq must be repeated three times to be accepted.
- If not written down, it's invalid.
- Talaq must be accepted by the wife to be effective.
- Talaq can be issued retroactively.

Misconceptions about Women's Rights in Talaq.

- Only men have the right to initiate talaq.
- Women cannot ask for divorce.
- Khula is not a real form of divorce.
- Talaq-e-Tafweez is not allowed.
- Women must return mahr in all cases of divorce
- A divorced woman cannot remarry.
- A woman who remarries after divorce is sinful.
- A woman must marry another man to return to her first husband (halala).
- A woman loses custody of her children immediately.
- Divorced women are a burden to society.

Misconceptions about Religious Rules & Culture.

- Triple talaq is encouraged in Islam.
- The Prophet (PBUH) frequently gave talaq.
- Divorce is always sinful in Islam.
- Islam favors men in all family matters.
- Talaq must be approved by family elders.
- Talaq means permanent shame for the woman.
- Only imams or scholars can pronounce talaq.
- A couple must live separately for talaq to be valid.
- Talaq means the woman is cursed or impure.

Guidance for Wives to Protect Marriage and Avoid Divorce (In the light of the Qur'an, Sunnah, and wisdom)

1. Maintain fear of Allah (Taqwa)

- Qur'an: "Whoever fears Allah, He will make a way out for him and provide for him from where he does not expect." (65:2)

2. Fulfil marital rights and responsibilities

- Qur'an: "Women have rights similar to the duties upon them, according to what is reasonable." (2:228)
- Hadith: "Each of you is a guardian and each of you will be questioned about what you are responsible for… a woman is the guardian of her husband's home." (Bukhari)

3. Speak gently and respectfully

- Qur'an: "Speak good words to people." (2:83)
- Hadith: "Gentleness beautifies everything it is part of." (Muslim)

4. Be grateful and appreciative

- Qur'an: "If you are grateful, I will surely give you more." (14:7)
- Hadith: "I was shown Hell and I saw that most of its inhabitants were women… because they are ungrateful to their husbands." (Bukhari)

5. Obey the husband in lawful matters

- Qur'an: "Men are protectors and maintainers of women." (4:34)

6. Give emotional support and comfort

- Qur'an: "He created spouses for you from among yourselves so that you may find peace in them." (30:21)
- Hadith: "This world is provision, and the best provision of it is a righteous woman." (Muslim)

7. Observe modesty and chastity

- Qur'an: "Guard your private parts." (24:31)

8. Do not compare your husband with others

- Qur'an: "Do not desire what Allah has given some of you over others." (4:32)
- Hadith: "Look at those below you, not those above you." (Muslim)

9. Protect the husband's honor and wealth in his absence

- Qur'an: "Righteous women are obedient and guard what Allah has commanded to be guarded in the husband's absence." (4:34)
- Hadith: "The best woman is one who pleases you when you look at her, obeys you when you command her, and protects herself and your wealth when you are absent." (Ahmad)

10. Be patient during hardships

- Qur'an: "Indeed, Allah is with the patient." (2:153)
- Hadith: "No fatigue, illness, or grief afflicts a Muslim except that Allah removes sins because of it." (Bukhari)

11. Help financially when needed (without force)

- Qur'an: "Help one another in righteousness and piety." (5:2)
- Hadith: "Hazrat Khadijah (RA) supported the Prophet ﷺ financially without complaint or demand."

12. Avoid backbiting and spreading marital matters

- Qur'an: "Do not backbite one another." (49:12)
- Hadith: "On the Day of Judgment, the worst people will be those who share marital secrets after intimacy." (Muslim)

13. Pray for your husband

- Qur'an: "Our Lord, grant us comfort of the eyes from our spouses and children." (25:74)
- Hadith: "Supplication strengthens relationships and brings blessings to the home."

14. Avoid unnecessary suspicion and jealousy

- Qur'an: "Avoid much suspicion; some suspicion is sinful." (49:12)
- Hadith: "False accusations and spying are disliked and sinful."

15. Dress well at home and maintain a pleasant manner

- Qur'an: "Do not display your beauty except to your husbands." (24:31)
- Hadith: "The world is enjoyment, and the best enjoyment is a righteous woman." (Muslim)

16. Support the husband's leadership in religion and worldly matters

- Qur'an: "Men are protectors and maintainers of women." (4:34)
- Hadith: "A wife is expected to respect her husband's leadership within Islamic limits."

17. Seek religious knowledge and act upon it

- Qur'an: "Are those who know equal to those who do not know?" (39:9)
- Hadith: "Seeking knowledge is obligatory for every Muslim." (Ibn Majah)

18. Try reconciliation before divorce

- Qur'an: "If you fear a dispute between them, appoint an arbitrator from his family and one from her family." (4:35)
- Hadith: "Among lawful things, divorce is the most disliked by Allah." (Abu Dawood)

Guidance for husbands to help preserve marriage and avoid divorce, inspired by the Qur'an, Sunnah, and wisdom:

1. Maintain Consciousness of Allah. (Taqwa)

- Qur'an: "And fear Allah, through whom you ask one another, and the wombs [that bore you]. Verily, Allah is ever over you, an Observer." (Qur'an, 4:1)

- Hadith: "The best of you are those who are best to their wives." (Tirmidhi)

2. Fulfill Marital Obligations with Sincerity.

- Qur'an: "And live with them in kindness." (Qur'an, 4:19)

- Hadith: "The most complete of the believers in faith is the one with the best character. And the best of you are those who are best to their women." (Tirmidhi)

3. Exhibit Kindness and Gentleness.

- Qur'an: "And speak to them a noble word." (Qur'an, 33:32)

- Hadith: "The strong man is not the one who can overpower others, but the one who controls himself when angry." (Sahih Muslim)

4. Communicate Respectfully and Constructively.

- Qur'an: "And speak to people in a gentle manner." (Qur'an, 2:83)

- Hadith: "A believer is not one who abuses, curses, or speaks in a rude manner." (Tirmidhi)

5. Express Gratitude and Appreciation.

- Qur'an: "And [remember] when your Lord proclaimed: 'If you give thanks [by accepting faith], I will give you more [of My Blessings]; but if you are thankless [i.e., ungrateful], verily My punishment is indeed severe.'" (Qur'an, 14:7)
- Hadith: "Whoever is not grateful to the people, he is not grateful to Allah." (Abu Dawood)

6. Provide Emotional Support.

- Qur'an: "And we created you in pairs." (Qur'an, 78:8)
- Hadith: "Your wife has a right over you, and you have a right over her." (Sahih Bukhari)

7. Preserve Loyalty and Trust.

- Qur'an: "And those who are [faithful] to their trusts and promises." (Qur'an, 23:8)

8. Exercise Patience and Restraint.

- Qur'an: "And be patient, for indeed, Allah is with the patient." (Qur'an, 8:46)
- Hadith: "Whoever is patient, Allah will grant him patience." (Sahih Bukhari)

9. Avoid Unwarranted Criticism and Comparison.

- Qur'an: "And do not wish for that by which Allah has made some of you exceed others." (Qur'an, 4:32)
- Hadith: "Do not compare yourselves to others but compare your deeds with the teachings of Islam." (Sahih Bukhari)

10. Observe Justice in All Matters.

- Qur'an: "O you who have believed, be persistently standing firm in justice, witnesses for Allah, even if it be against yourselves or parents and relatives." (Qur'an, 4:135)
- Hadith: "Fear Allah and be just to your wives." (Sahih Muslim)

11. Fulfill Financial Responsibilities.

- Qur'an: "Let the rich man spend according to his means; and the man whose provision is limited, let him spend according to what Allah has given him." (Qur'an, 65:7)
- Hadith: "It is a responsibility of the husband to provide for his wife's maintenance." (Sahih Muslim)

12. Promote Religious Growth.

- Hadith: "The best of you are those who are best to their women, and the best of you are those who help their wives in religious matters." (Tirmidhi)

13. Avoid Using Divorce as a Threat.

- Hadith: "Do not divorce except for the most serious reasons." (Sunan Abu Dawood)

14. Involve Her in Family Decisions.

- Qur'an: "And consult them in the matter." (Qur'an, 3:159)
- Hadith: "The Prophet (PBUH) consulted his wives in all affairs." (Sahih Bukhari)

15. Respect your wife's dignity and privacy

- Qur'an: "Live with them in kindness." (4:19)

- Hadith: "On the Day of Judgment, the worst person will be the one who shares his wife's private matters." (Muslim)

16. Give time and companionship importance

- Qur'an: "He created spouses from among yourselves so that you may find peace in them, and He placed love and mercy between you." (30:21)

17. Maintain Intimacy with Love and Consideration.

- Qur'an: "And those who guard their private parts except from their wives or those their right hands possess..." (Qur'an, 23:5-6)
- Hadith: "The most virtuous of you are those who are most gentle with their wives." (Ibn Majah)

18. Be Willing to Acknowledge Mistakes.

- Qur'an: "And those who, when they commit an immorality or wrong themselves [by sin], remember Allah and seek forgiveness for their sins..." (Qur'an, 3:135)
- Hadith: "The one who apologizes when he is wrong is the one who is closest to Allah." (Sunan Abu Dawood)

19. Refrain from Cultural Injustices.

- Qur'an: "And do not let the hatred of a people prevent you from being just." (Qur'an, 5:8)
- Hadith: "Islam does not permit any form of oppression, whether cultural or otherwise." (Sunan Ibn Majah)

20. Seek Reconciliation and Counsel When Needed.

- Qur'an: "If you fear a breach between them, appoint an arbitrator from his family and an arbitrator from her family." (Qur'an, 4:35)
- Hadith: "If there is a disagreement between husband and wife, an attempt should be made to reconcile them." (Sahih Bukhari)

The verses and hadiths mentioned above are clear and simple about how the conduct and character ease marital relationships. Life is very important and it is a mix of planned and unplanned events. Sometimes it is unpredictable and chaotic, but that is the nature of life. The system of pairs is designed universally: birds, animals, humans, and even atoms join with other atoms to become stable. As the author of this book I advise readers to read, understand, and reflect upon these teachings in your marital life. Your marital life should not be decided by so-called unreasonable customs of people, but should be based on reasonable causes. Both husband and wife should believe in patience, understanding, and companionship. I am ending my book on a key lesson of Prophet Ibrahim (peace be upon him) When Prophet Ibrahim left Hazrat Hajar (peace be upon her) and infant Hazrat Ismail in the empty desert of Makkah by Allah's command, she asked:

"Has Allah commanded you to do this?"

When he replied yes, she said:

"Then Allah will not abandon us."

www.ingramcontent.com/pod-product-compliance
Lightning Source LLC
Chambersburg PA
CBHW050022170726
48282CB00025B/511
* 9 7 8 9 3 3 4 2 6 3 5 5 8 *